"I love Ephesus.

Through my years of guiding, I've always tried
to guide with the touch of this love.
In this book, as you go through the beloved city,
Ephesus, step by step, I hope you, too will feel that
you're being guided by somebody
who cares and loves.
I would like to extend my gratitudes to all of
those who had contributed to the realization
of this book."

EDITOR
TUNÇAY YURTSEVER

AUTHOR
MEHLİKA SEVAL

ART DIRECTOR
CEMALETTİN MUTVER

DESIGN
GÜLŞEN SEMİZ

PHOTOGRAPHS
MERİÇ AYTANÇ
TUNCER CEBECİ
İSA ÇELİK
ŞEMSİ GÜNER
AHMET KUZİK

COLOR SEPERATIONS
MAS FİLM

PRINTED BY
MAS MATBAACILIK A.Ş.

TYPESETTING BY
KROS FOTODİZGİ

MİNYATÜR PUBLICATIONS 14/B

İSTANBUL TURKEY

NO: 89. 34. Y0044. 56
ISBN 975. 7647. 05-5

LET'S VISIT

EPHESUS

MİNYATÜR PUBLICATIONS

No. 14/B

GALERİ MİNYATÜR MEŞRUTİYET CAD. 93/A 80050 TEPEBAŞI - İSTANBUL/TURKEY
PHONES: (9.1) 149 46 90 - 151 04 72 - 152 09 86

B I B L I O G R A P H Y

E. Akurgal	Ancient Civilisations and Ruins of Turkey, İstanbul 1969
M. Bayral	Secret Ephesus. İzmir 1985
Everett Blake	Biblical Sites In Turkey
B.F. Deutsch	Our Lady of Ephesus. Milwaukee 1965
A.G. Edmonds	İstanbul 1982
S. Erdemgil	Ephesus, İstanbul 1986
C. Foss	Ephesus After Antiquity: A late Antique, Byzantine and Turkish City, Cambridge University Press 1979
H. Hamilton	Mythology, New York 1962
Heredotos	Herodot Tarihi Çev. M. Ökmen, İstanbul 1973
O.F.A. Meinardus	St. Paul In Ephesus. Athens 1973
Ü. Önen	Ephesus Ruins and Museum, İzmir 1983
C. Şakir	Asia Minor, İzmir 1971
C. Şakir	Merhaba Anadolu, İstanbul 1980
S. Türkoğlu	Efes'de 3000 Yıl, İstanbul 1986
R.E. Wycherley	Antik Çağda Kentler Nasıl Kuruldu, Çev. N. Nirven N. Başgelen İstanbul 1986
J.E. Zimmerman	Dictionary of Classical Mythology, New York 1966

TURKEY

Occupying the whole of classical Asia Minor (Anatolia) and a small portion of Eastern Thrace in Europe, Turkey has a total area of roughly 296.000 sq. mi. It is bounded on the north by the Black Sea, on the east by Russia and by Iran, on the south by Iraq, Syria and the Mediterranean Sea, and on the west by the Aegean Sea. In Europe it has land frontiers with Greece and Bulgaria.

It is, for the most part, an elevated plateau enclosed by mountains on all sides but the west. The Coastline totals 8400 km. (5252 miles). As for the mountains, the highest is Ağrı Dağı at 5165 m (Mnt. Ararat). Going from west to east, the climatic regions of Turkey are as follow:

MARMARA

This includes the European part of the country, Eastern Thrace, and the southern part of the Sea of Marmara. On the European side, the topography is rolling steppeland, and low hills, good for grazing and farming and industry. On the southern shore of the Sea of Marmara there are low hills and higher mountains. The land is very rich, excellent for agriculture. The average temperture is 14°C.

EGE (Aegean)

Higher mountains which run parallel to each other from east to west are separated from each other by meandering rivers. The mild climate of the sea can penetrate inland, making the whole area the most agreeable place to live. Figs, olives, grapes, citrus trees, tobacco fields, cotton fields, and sun flower fields constantly change the view as one travels in this region. The average air temperature for the year is 17 °C.

AKDENİZ (Mediterranean)

The great Toros (Taurus) mountain range runs parallel to the coastline of the Mediterranean. In some parts the slopes of the mountain dives into the sea and in some parts, as if protecting the fertile fields, the mountains encircle the valleys. The temperature is slightly warmer than of the Aegean region but it is always a nice contrast to see the snow capped mountains almost year round from the sea, where the sea temperature will be not less than 22-23°C. Vegetables, fruits, and cotton are produced in this region.

ORTA ANADOLU (Central Anatolia)

Surrounded by high mountain ranges, the high Anatolian plateau is spotted with snow capped peaks. The land is mostly rolling steppe, though, good for growing wheat and raising sheep. The rainfall is usually in the spring and fall. The average temperature is around 11°C.

KARADENİZ (Black Sea Area)

The coastline is 1700 km (1000 miles). The narrow strip of land which is squeezed between the high range of mountains and the Black Sea can not help but be very generous when the moderate temperature and the right amount of rainfall is added to the typical characteristics of the region. Fishing, tea, and hazel nut production are the major activities of the people. The best cooks of the country come from this area, as well.

GÜNEYDOĞU ANADOLU (Southeast Anatolia)

The rivers Tigris and Euphrates run through this region. The new project under construction is partially completed and once dry, rocky valleys are now or will be properly irrigated to create one of the agriculturally richer corners of the country. The 20% of oil which is being consumed in Turkey is drilled from the wells around Batman thus the region contributes a lot to the Turkish economy. The rainfall is very scarce (382 mm per year) and the average temperature is around 16°C.

DOĞU ANADOLU (Eastern Anatolia)

Mountainous and wildly beautiful landscape takes one from the peaks of Mount Ararat, which is covered with glaciers, to warm valleys where grape and tobacco can be grown. The average temperature is a cool 9°C but varying between 38°C and -45°C. Raising livestock and growing wheat are the main sources of income for the people living here. The socially and economically neglected image of the region has been fast changing in the last decade.

ATATÜRK

Atatürk, Mustafa Kemal, the founder and the first president of the Turkish Republic, was born in 1881 in Selânik. When he was a small child, he lost his father and was raised by his mother, Zübeyde Hanım. He had his education in the military schools by his own choice, in spite of his mother's discontent. He was a very successful student. His math teacher, whose name was also Mustafa, one day said, "My boy, your name is Mustafa, so is mine... we should change this. There must be a difference between us. From now on your name will be Mustafa Kemal..." Kemal meaning mature and perfect.

Atatürk is the national hero of the Turks. He always fought victoriously ageinst the enemy, starting with the lowest rank, at Tripoly, at Gallipoli in the Ist World War, on the Eastern front, and, finally, in the War of Independence which he commanded. The quality that saved his heroism from personal ambition was his patriotism.

Atatürk, in the widest meaning of the words, was a changer of society, a revolutionary, and a reformer. He had a realistic outlook and power of thought and saw very well the nature of the Ottoman society in which he had passed his childhood and youth. He knew the social institutions and the values of the deteriorating empire. After the foundation of an independent Turkish state (1923), with the power of his great spirit he attacked the institutions that had for centuries been an obstacle to our progress in development.

— The establishment of the Republic, the abolition of the Sultanate
— The establishment of a secular state, the removal of the Caliphate
— The acceptence of the Code of Civil law, the outruling of the Islamic Law
— The changing of the Arabic script to Latin letters

— The legal ban on veil and fez
  Veil was associated with fanatic tradition, which under the name of Islamic
  tradition did not allow the women to "See" the world through their own
  eyes. Similar mentality had forced the woman not to take her proper role
  in society. Such discrimination, according to Atatürk, was paralyzing one-
  half of the nation. To have a "healthy society" the women, like the men,
  had to be the enlightening and constructive member of her community.
  The ban on veil was giving the women pride and the responsibility of being a citizen who should take part in the development of the Turkish
  nation.
  The fez versus the hat was representative of the eastern mentality versus
  the western mentality. The ban on fez was an introduction to the new
  values which would rescue the Turkish culture from superstitious belief.
— The emancipation of women.
  Each one of these is an important and honored stage in the great reform
movement led by Atatürk. National language, and national history movements
were the beginning for the rebirth of Turkish pride.
  The ideal of his reforming spirit, which is now shared by every single Türk,
was to bring society to the level of contemporary civilization and to ever
preserve our national character.
  Atatürk, with all his qualities and activities, was a hero who can rarely be
seen in the history of the world in the way in which he realized his ideals.
  The Turkish people love him, respect him and follow him.
  Atatürk, the father of the Turks...

EPHESUS, THE CITY OF THE BEE.

EPHESUS, THE CITY OF THE MOTHER GODDESS, ARTEMIS

One thing common to both titles is they are both related to the Amazons, the female warriors whose traditions in Ephesus have long lived in the legends, stone carvings, and literary works of the city. In a hymn to Artemis Challimachus writes,

"The Amazons, in their ritual dances around the altar of the Mother Goddess, Artemis, tossed their spears and clashed their cymbals."

The historian Strabo, in his book, writes that the city was named after an Amazon queen. The name of the queen was Apasas. In the native Anatolian language spoken then in the Hittite Kingdom, Apasas meant 'bee".

When the first coinage was minted in the Fifth Century B.C. and until coins were no longer minted in the name of Ephesus, for nearly eight hundred years after, the coins of Ephesus had a bee on one side showing that Apasas, the bee, was associated with the city.

The Amazons were the first ones to settle here but they were not the ones who developed the town into the city which would turn out to be a trade and religious center for centuries to come.

Androklos was not happy with the city he was living in, it was too crowded. He wanted to 'found' a new town. The tradition, in those times, was to get permission for such an undertaking from the oracles. Androklos did as tradition demanded, he went to the Delphic Oracle. The Oracle gave him permission and also prophesied the location where he should establish the city. A fish, a fire, and a boar were supposed to show Androklos the place.

Androklos and his friends were a bit hopeless about the prophesy, how were they to find these three odd things at the same place? But they had to trust the Oracle so they decided to give it a try. They set off in the Aegean Sea. Their small boat stopped in every possible bay but they could not find what they were seeking. They finally thought they had had enough adventure. They would have to go back for a crowded home is better than no home.

The last night out they wanted to have a feast to cheer them up before they started back. The fish they had just caught in the sea were to be their meal and they put the fresh fish in the pan. But the fish were very fresh, they jumped from the pan, scattered the flames, and set the forest where they planned to have their feast on fire. A boar, which had been hiding behind some bushes, was frightened by the fire and began to run away. Androklos shot the boar and discovered where he should establish his new city.

The fish must have represented it must be near the sea. Ephesus was by the sea. Where there is a boar the land is fertile, it likes to feed itself the easy way - on farms. In the fields around Ephesus if you were to put a stick in the ground and if the stick has even a little bit of life left to it then it will sprout within a couple of weeks.

The Oracle was right, Androklos had to 'found' his city where the land was fertile, by the sea, in EPHESUS.

In the Eleventh Century B.C., the Carians and the Lelegs, the native population, accepted the colonist — provided that the native tradition of the Mother Goddess was respected. For four hundred years the descendents of Androklos, the natives of the region, and many more who came from all over Anatolia hoping to get their share of the wealth lived in this first city of Ephesus, which then was located by the sea. The Ephesians cleverly used the location of the city and its well-protected harbour. The products of Anatolia coming on the trade routes (which started in Mesopotamia) could easily be shipped out from Ephesus and the products of the islands in the Aegean were brought into Anatolia through Ephesus. Due to this trade the city became very rich and the people wanted to dedicate a temple to their Mother Goddess, Artemis.

The temple had to be larger and more beautiful than any other temple ever built before and, once the temple was finished, it did reflect their great wealth. The Ephesians were very proud of it until they checked their records of expenses. They realized then that more money had been spent on the temple than they had intended. So they had to use the temple to make more money, to recoup their expenses. Of course, nobody was openly admitting to the idea but the solution they found was novel. They would honor the Mother Goddess and make some moneyThey made an anouncement to the whole known world. They said, "If you believe in a mother goddess, it does not matter by which name you call her, then remember the Mother Goddess has a house here in Ephesus. This is the biggest house ever built in the name of any one mother goddess and, if she is living here, she must be protecting her house herself. If she is protecting her house then whatever goes into the temple will be equally protected. So, if you have valuable things which need to be protected, like gold, money, treasures, and etc., then do not hesitate for a second. Leave it in the safe hands of your Mother Goddess. Not only will she protect them for you but she will be so thrilled with your trust in her that she would like to give you a gift at the end of each year to show you her gratitude."

The gift, of course, was nothing more than an offer of interest. People, ever since they began to walk on their own two feet, have wanted something more than what they already had. So, from Egypt, Mesopotamia, Anatolia, Greece... people started pouring into the temple with their valuables. With the speculation of the capital the Ephesians grew richer and richer. But the popularity of Ephesus attracted not only the traders but greedy kings, as well.

In the Sixth Century, King Croesus of Lydia attacked Ephesus. The king must have thought he should not kill off the hen which laid the golden eggs so he treated the Ephesians very nicely. In fact, he encouraged them to build a new city, not too far away from the first one, which was no longer by the harbour. The River Kaystros had silted in the bay of the first city, as it still does today. The second city was then built closer to the temple.

The Ephesians and other Ionic cities, like the rest of Anatolia, were confronted with another threat in 547 B.C. The Persians were coming. As they passed over Anatolia they left no two stones standing on top of another. The Ephesians realized that if they were to resist the Persians they would have no future. They had to avoid this danger cleverly, they could not afford to lose their temple, the house of their holy mother, and the bank. They also could

The Amazons '' They tossed their spears
and clashed their cymbols''

not afford to be considered treasonous to the Ionic Confederation. The solution they found was another example of their genius. The Ephesians called the Panionic Confederation together. The cities of this region, known as Ionia, were all members of the Confederation. The Ephesians said, "The Persians are coming. We, certainly, all want to fight against them. But if we all fight then we might neglect the Mother Goddess. In that case, her fury might be worse than that of the Persians. Somebody should do the fighting and somebody else should do the worshipping. Since we, the Ephesians, are closer to her house we had better do the worshipping and you do the fighting." The Temple of Artemis,this generous bank, was too precious for any of them to neglect. The offer was unanimously accepted and Ephesus was made neutral. Ephesus maintained its economic power and continued its trade and cultural relations while the other Ionic cities under the rule of Persia were buried in the dark ages.

The excitement in Ephesus grew worse on May 21,356 B.C. They knew how to impress the Lydian kings, they knew how to trick the Ionians and the Persians, they knew many clever ways of surviving. But what could they do about an idiot, a man named Herostratos who wanted his name to be written in history? Herostratos burned the temple. Was Artemis not protecting her

Androclos.
The legendary
founder of Ephesus.

Androclos chasing the boar
to establish the location
of the city, Ephesus.

house any more? Should people think that Ephesus was no longer a safe place for their Mother Goddess or their money? Would this be the end of business in Ephesus?

No. The Ephesians were more clever than that. They would not let one terrible fire destroy their reputation and create doubtful ideas about their Mother, Artemis. Soon, they came up with a very dramatic story... on that night of fire, the Mother Goddess was not in the Temple. She had a more important mission. She had been in Macedonia, helping the mother of Alexander the

13

Great with the delivery of the baby Alexander. Of course, who else but a Mother Goddess would help a 'Great' person like Alexander come into this world?

Naturally, it would be the Mother, the Goddess, Artemis. As soon as she completed her mission Artemis had returned to her house. It was, in other words, as safe as ever to be used as a bank and to carry on contributing to the religious importance of the city.

Everyone, including Alexander, believed in this dramatic lie. To clear his conscience, Alexander called upon the Ephesians and said, "You do not need to worry. I will restore the Temple in such a beautiful way that you will not even remember what the old temple was like and, I will have my name written on the Temple."

The Temple of Artemis.
The Temple of Artemis had to be larger and more beautiful
than any other temple ever built before.

The Ephesians, knowing that he was feeling guilty, wanted something more from Alexander... and they did not want to have his name on their temple. The Ephesians answered him, "A God can not build a house for another God." This was nothing but flattery. Alexander felt great, though. The Ephesians had deified him, so the city deserved much more;they were not going to pay taxes anymore and they would be given the necessary assistance to complete the Temple and... his name was not going to be put on the house of another God.

The glory that the Ephesians enjoyed during the reign of Alexander did not last during the reign of his General. Lysimachos changed the name of the city

to Arsinoe (the name of his wife). The Ephesians did not like this at all. They showed their discontent by not moving to the new city which he built as the third city of Ephesus. This is the city which the whole world admires today. The city was built in the best possible way. Much money was spent for the construction. In order to find funds for the foundation of the new city, Lysimachos raised the taxes of all the cities under his rule. Nobody liked him. In fact, when he died a writer proclaimed, "Nobody but his dog had mourned for his death." Eventually, the Ephesians did move to the other location.. for

The Temple of Hadrian.
The Roman emperors contributed
a lot to the beauty of the city.

the third time in their history... and remained there for nearly eight hundred years.

During the Roman Period, Ephesus became the largest metropolis and the capital of the Eastern Provinces of the Roman Empire. The population was around 250.000 for more than two centuries. The Roman emperors visited the city and restored and built new edifices, adding more and more fame and architectural beauty to be admired - even many centuries later.

During the First Century A.D., christianity gained popularity. St. Paul, St. John, and the Virgin Mary lived in the city. The Bible was referring to Ephesus. The Romans were taking pride in contributing more and more to the beauty of the city. The Ephesians were enjoying the memories of the past when they had been able to create a goddess, start a bank, trick the people in many ways so they could protect and beautify their city. Christianity was finding many followers and Ephesus became one of the Seven Churches of Asia, where the mother of Jesus was given a divine personality. But, even with all this fame and glory, the Ephesians were helpless against the smallest of creatures. The mosquitoes were the last invaders of Ephesus and the first ones to beat them. The threat of malaria coming from the silted harbour forced the Ephesians

The River God.
The River Kaystros had silted
in the bay of Ephesus.

to move out from this beautiful city in the middle of the Sixth Century A.D. The Ephesians then moved to the fourth location where the Basilica of St. John was built.

THE RESERVOIR

The water was coming to Ephesus on four aquaducts. One of the source of water is as far as 42,5 kms. Each one of the aquaducts had a different rate of flow of the water. Varying between 61 liters/second to only 4,2 leters/second, but never the less, even in mid summer when there was no rain for more than six months the city had never suffered of lack of water.

The circular building by the two big plane trees to the left of the State Agora was the reservoir. The water was reserved there, filtered through coal and pebbles and then through the amazing water system of the city, the water was distributed to the houses.

Only those houses which were placed in a level lower than the reservoir had running water. Obviously they had no pumping system, but they were useing the law of gravity to get the water go up to the houses on the hill side.

Though most of the time overgrown with the weeds around, it is still possible to see the plumming system of the city on the ground around the State Agora.

A Stock of Pipes.

Aquaduct.
The water came to Ephesus
via four aquaducts, one of which
is traced 42.5 kms. away from the city.

THE STATE AGORA

In his book, Heredotes quotes the Persian king, Kyros, "I have never been scared of those people (Ionians) who met at a place designated for them in the middle of the town. There, they were giving promises and lying to each other."

As any despot would have, Kyros had not sympathized with the institution of liberal minds and free communication but, at least, he was able to associate with the "agora" as a distinct symbol of a certain social mentality.

Actually, the agora was not just made up of public buildings; it was the place where the heart of the town was beating. The structure of the agora used to be very simple. It was a wide space which could be used for various activities. A lecturer could have had his audience listen to him there as he was talking about the "virtues of honesty" or another such philosophical subject. There could have been an announcement made about the emancipation of a slave. A king could have been there listening to the problems of his people. There could have been cymbals being played at a corner to carry on religious rituals. But, to change the agora into a market place took only a few big wooden tables, portable counters, added to the "stage" of activity.

As the cities grew bigger and other buildings were added —like an odeom for music, a town hall for official administration, sophisticated temples for religious rituals...-the number of activities for which the agora was used decreased. But the agora was never decreased in importance to the people.

The agora was even classified within itself as to what purpose it would be used. If the agora were used for trade, it would be called the "commercial agora". If it were used for formal activities, it would be called the "state agora".

Along with the specified function of the agora, the architecture of the agora took on a specific form, as well. In accordance with the city development plan of Ionia (Hippodomic Plan) to fit in the parallel streets which crossed each other at right angles, the agora became rectangular buildings with colonnaded

The State Agora
... where the courts were held and the
political speaches were given.

galleries on the sides, with a courtyard in the center, and an altar in the middle of the courtyard.

The area where you can see a stack of pipes in front of Varius Bath is the state agora of Ephesus. This is the place where courts were held, elections were made, and important political speeches were given.

Criminals and "dirty" people were not allowed to enter the state agora. This tradition was due to the sacred nature of the building. In addition, the artistic decoration of the agora was closely related to both religious and political

The rectangular temple
in the middle of the State Agora
is thought to have been dedicated to Isis.

events. The rectangular courtyard of the state agora was surrounded by colonnaded galleries on two sides. To suit the political nature of the agora the marble-paved courtyard and the galleries were decorated with the statues of the members of the Advisory Council "Ecclesia". The statues of rich Ephesians were also erected in the agora to honor those who had subsidized the expenses of the construction or the restoration of the official building of the town. The rectangular temple in the middle of the courtyard is thought to have been dedicated to Isis (an Egyptian goddess) or to the Roman Emperor Augustos.

The state agora was built on the necropole (cemetery) and the Sacred Road of the Archaic Period. They can now be seen 2-3 meters below the agora.

An inscription carved on one of the marble benches found in the agora suggests that part of the courtyard in late antiquity may have been used for ceremonial purposes by the clergy of the Christians.

Varius Bath.

THE
BASILICA

The well restored colonnaded gallery of the state agora was the Basilica. The two rows of columns had divided the Basilica into three naves. At the end of the hall was an apse with an altar in front of it. The walls were faced with marble and there were laws, regulations, and the name "Artemis" on the marble. In the Fourth Century A.D., the building was "Christianized" and the name of Artemis was erased from the inscription. Crosses were carved on the foreheads of the statues of Emperor Augustos and his wife, Livia, to whom the portico had originally been dedicated.

Emperor Augustos.
Crosses were carved on the foreheads
of the Statues to Christianize them.

THE SIDE ENTRANCE TO THE ODEON

As one walks into the Odeon, looking at the few symbols there, it is easy to "see" the summary of the history of Ephesus.

On the wall there sit the bull-headed capitals of the columns which were used to decorate the Basilica. The curved horn figures representing the Ionic Order show the fine taste of this town which was once the most powerful of all the Ionic cities.

The trade the Ephesians carried out with the eastern part of Anatolia had an undeniable influence on their wealth. However, on the trade routes not only material products are exchanged, the cultures are transmitted, as well. The bull, in the Anatolian Culture since the 7th millenium B.C., stands for power and superiority. The Ephesians decorated their Basilica with these bull-headed capitals as an implication of the powerful role of the Basilica.

At the entrance of the Odeon, on the center of the gate, there stands a cross. The Odeon, itself, is a Roman period construction.

The Ionic capital, adorned with a bull head, sitting on the wall of the Roman building, which has a cross on the gate, can be interpreted as follows: This Ionic town had carried on close relations with the East and was influenced by it. Later, Ephesus came under the rule of the Romans. The Roman city became Christian at a later point.

The side entrance to the Odeon.
Bull headed Ionic Capital
sitting on the wall of a
Roman Construction which has
a cross on the entrance.

THE ODEON

This small theater was built aproximately 150 A.D. by Publius Vedius Antonius. It was used as a concert hall, as well as a bouleuterion (Council Chamber).

In the antique sites, in order to visualize what a building had looked like, you must use your imagination. But if you let your imagination run wild you might end up with something which has no similarity to how it actually was. Therefore, in order to truly visualize what this odeon, (which seated 1400 people) had looked like, we have to base our imaginations on some criteria.

If you look in the orchestra, you will see that there is no drainage. That means that rain water was not falling in the orchestra so there must have been a roof at the top. If there were a roof, there must have been windows to let the sunlight in.

We can now put some things together... since we are talking about a Roman Period construction, we are probably talking about their most popular form of construction, the arch form. So the windows must have been arched, closed with beautiful colors of stained glass, letting a dim sunlight project over the stage from different angles at different hours of the day as the sun went around the building.

While the windows were supporting the roof at one end, the stage building (the skena) was supporting the roof at the other end. The skena must not have been as high as the top of the windows, though, so the roof would be tilted toward the agora to allow water to run down. The stage building was faced with marble and decorated with the statues of those who had performed on the stage. One can imagine a statue of a poet with a scroll in his hand, a dignified look on his face... he'd be reciting his poetry. Another statue would be that of a dancer in a very graceful pose, dancing to the music being played in the orchestra. Or one can imagine the statues of the musicians, each holding a musical instrument, a golden lyre or a Pan flute.

If you now look at the auditorium (the cavea), you will see lion paws on the stairways. Lion paws were a symbol of power and aristocracy. You can imagine the aristocrats in their burgundy togas with golden chains hanging from their necks. They would be leaning back on those beautiful marble seats... some enjoying, some pretending that they were enjoying, the performances which were taking place on the stage.

The Odeon.

THE TOWN HALL (PRYTANEION)

When one walks through the perfect arch which gives access to the Odeon, there stand the Imperial Temple and the Town Hall. Architecture, during each period of history, has been used to evaluate the needs, mentality and values of the people. If one looks at this big complex from this point of view, a few characteristics of the Ephesians can be traced by the plan of the construction.

The two big columns stand in front of the temple of the Town Hall and, right adjacent to the temple, the marble courtyard belonging to the administrative part of the Town Hall. When the administrative and the religious departments are side by side the interpretation can easily be made that they must have had a theocratic form of government. Religion had something to do with administration and administration had something to do with religion. However, we know very well that the Ephesians would never allow religion to rule over them. After all, they had used even their Temple of Artemis as much as a bank as a sanctuary.

Also, when they refused to listen to St. Paul they were scared more of losing their way of making money than of changing their religious beliefs. So we know they were not too keen on religion.

The inscriptions on the columns in front of the temple state the laws related to the ministries of Ephesus, the reason why those laws were inscribed there and not on the other columns of the Town Hall is because they were trying to give a message to the gods... ''Gods, if you want to interfere with our administration you can do so, but, only so much because these are the laws by which we run our city.''

Looking at the administrative part of the complex other speculations can be made about the way Ephesians ran their city. The excavations on the slope of the hill behind the marble courtyard are the rooms. The number of these rooms are about four times more than what would be expected in a town hall. The reason for having so many rooms is because they needed all those bureaus to carry on their bureaucracy.

The Prytaneion was constructed in the III Century B.C. and restored and rebuilt many more times after that until it got its final shape during the early Ist Century A.D.

Though the town was then being ruled by the Romans, the tastes of the Ephesians for art and for vulgar sports like gladiator fights did not match the tastes of the Romans. The urge for creating beauty with simplicity remained in the Anatolian Ephesians and was reflected in their construction. For this

The Town Hall.

very important building of their town they chose simple Doric and Ionic order. As if Michelangelo had wanted to praise this mentality of achieving beauty through simplicity he said, centuries later, "Wherever there is too much work, there is less art."

When Prometheus granted mankind fire, it was still up to man to find a practical way of lighting it. The evolution of man can, in fact, be traced by their success in facilitating the first strike of fire. The achievement of this

The eternal fire of Ephesus was kept
alive here for centuries.

success did not come quickly, thus fire was very difficult to start and it was made taboo so no one could go close to it and turn it off. The tradition then was to keep the fire alive as long as the town existed. Ages later, it became very easy to light fires but the traditions were not so easy to forget. So, the tradition of having a sacred fire was kept but with a reversed meaning. It was then believed that a town should have a sacred fire which was to be kept alive to ensure an eternal life for the town. In other words, at first it was:

There should be a fire in the town as long as the town existed.

later it was:

The town will exist as long as there is an eternal fire in the town.

The eternal fire of Ephesus was kept alive for centuries in the center of the Town Hall at Hestai's Sacred Hearth to symbolize the existence of their city. The Turkish National Anthem cries out this same tradition:

"Have no doubt, our flag will fly over our sky.

Until the last hearth of my country is put out..."

The Ionic columns
of the Town Hall
"Creating beauty
with simplicity."

In the IVth Century A.D., Ephesus lost the status for which the Town Hall had stood, namely, Free City (Civitas Libera). Then the columns with the inscriptions of the detailed code of ethics and administrative regulations which stood up for seven centuries (3rd Century B.C. - 4th Century A.D.) with dignity and demanding superiority were reduced to nothing more than a marble quarry.

The diverse values of the 4th Century regarded the Town Hall not as the construction of existence but as material for further construction. The masons of the Skolastikia Bath, therefore, did not have far to go to find the marble they needed.

The T
The diverse values of the 4th
not as the cons
but as material fo

Hall.
ry regarded the Town Hall,
n of existence
re construction.

Walking down on the original marble pavement of the antique street, a few meters away from the Town Hall, there is a hole in the ground with four (used to be four, now there are two) iron rings around it. They used to place a pole with a torch on top in this hole, tying the pole to the rings. They would light the street at night with this portable lamp pole and set it aside during the day. In the residential section of the town, the street lights were attached to the columns on the side of the streets but, in this upper part of the town, they put their lights in the center of the streets for security purposes - so nobody could come on horseback and dash into the state part of the town.

At the end of the road, before the Domitian Square, there stand two statue bases facing each other. The one on the left hand side has the medical symbol with a tripod and a snake around the legs of a table and the other one, on the right hand side, has the symbol of pharmacy, with a tripod, a mortar, and a pestle. The building behind the medical symbol (the caduceus) is built with big blocks of stones. The architecture of the building does not reveal anything as to what it might have been used for. However, since these symbols, related to medicine and pharmacy, were found here it is most possible that it was a medical treatment center.

On the Aegean Islands and on the western coast of Anatolia there were many "health centers", Ausculapions. Some were big, some were small complexes but they all had similar means of treatment.

The treatment began in the entrance. Over the two symbols of medicine and pharmacy there stood two signs. One said, "DEATH CAN NOT ENTER" and the other read, "NO WILLS WILL BE READ HERE". These quotations were good enough to make the patient believe that he would not die at the hospital. After the patient was accepted to the hospital, he would be asked to sacrifice an animal. The sacrific ceremony was held in a very holy atmosphere to make the patient believe that he had done what was needed for God and that now it was God's turn to give him his health back.

In the next step, the patient was taken into an underground tunnel. Not knowing how long he would be there or how far he was supposed to go, he would start walking in that dark tunnel. All of a sudden, from the small holes above, he would hear a 'divine' voice calling upon him saying, "You'll get well. You'll get well." The patient would think it was God calling upon him and he would be totally relieved, thinking, "Oh! Good God knows that I'm here. He will definitely help me get well." In other words, the patient would develop confidence in himself, in the hospital, and, the most important thing, in God. This was where the mind started working over matter.

The patient was later taken into a small chamber where he'd be given some tranquilizers and be put to sleep. Then, the very same doctor with the 'divine' voice would come in the room. This time, not using his 'divine' voice, he'd whisper in the ear of the sleeping patient... he'd say, "If you really want to get well, you'd better take my advice." His advice would either be taking part in a sports activity... which is now called physiotherapy or he would advise taking part in drama activity... which is now called psychodrama, or the patient would be advised to take a bath in a sacred water. Those 'sacred waters' have been analyzed and were found to be rich with one mineral or another which would be therapeutic for certain illnesses. When the patient woke up he would think that he had had a dream and had seen God in his dream so he'd do as he was advised and he would get well.

Supposedly, the list of the names of those who entered the hospital were identical to the names of those who came back out of it alive. Certainly it was not a miraculous treatment which was responsible for this success. It was the very cautious doctors who did the first check-up for the admittance for if the patient seemed to be fatally ill then the patient had no chance of getting in the hospital.

In fact, the reason for the snake as the symbol of medicine goes back to this tradition. A legend says that there was a man who needed to go into one of these hospitals. The doctor at the entrance, however, thought that he was

The rings to tie up the street light pole.

fatally ill and did not accept him. Knowing the tradition, the patient knew he was going to die and thought that instead of waiting for his death, he might as well commit suicide and get it over with immediately. He did not know how to go about killing himself though. As he was walking away from the hospital, he saw a snake drinking milk from a cup and spitting the milk back out in the same cup. The patient, thinking that his milk must be poisonous, grabbed the cup and drank the milk. To the surprise of the man, and the doctor (who was keeping an eye on the patient), the patient started getting well. It was realized that one way of fighting illness was to take the right amount of venom in the body, vaccination! The snake was then made the symbol of medicine.

THE DOMITIAN SQUARE

Past the symbols of medicine and pharmacy, there is the largest square of Ephesus. The area is surrounded with fountains, monuments, and colonnaded sidewalks.

Symbol of Pharmacy.

Symbol of Medicine.

The Domician Square.
The largest square of Ephesus.

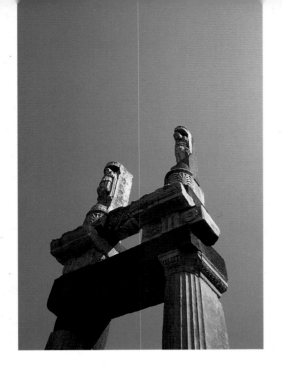

THE TEMPLE OF DOMITIAN

On the left, the arched-formed construction was the building dedicated to the Emperor Domitian (81-91 A.D.). This Roman emperor was a megalomaniac. He would always use the superlative forms of adjectives to describe himself. He would say, "I am the richest, the biggest, the greatest, the most magnificent." As if these words were not enough to describe just how big and great he was, he would also call even his most modest-scaled accommodation "the temple of Domitian", pretending to be a god.

When Ephesus was granted the temple wardenship by Emperor Domitian, this temple was built and dedicated to him. To suit his meglomania, the Ephesians tried their best to give a colossal appearance to the construction.

The arched-formed substructure was built to elevate the land level to enable the formation of a terrace of 100 by 50 meters. The temple was then built on this terrace and could be seen from every point in Ephesus. The temple was a colonnaded one, 13 columns on the sides and 8 in the front and in the back. There stood an altar in front of the temple. Arms, soldiers, and fighting scenes... all those which are still being considered as symbols of power... decorated the altar. The huge statue of Domitian had added another impressive image to the whole complex. Only the head and an arm of the statue were found. The arm piece, from the knuckles to the elbow, measured approximately 180 cm. (6 ft.) It is located in the Izmir Archeological Museum. This measurement suggests that the statue must have been 6-7 meters tall (about 22 ft.)

The substructure was surrounded with a row of three sets of columns. The columns in the middle row were decorated with soldier figures. Supposedly they were to protect the temple.

After Emperor Domitian was assassinated by one of his servants, the Ephesians did not care less about him any longer. With an attitude of 'The king is dead, viva the new king', they re-dedicated the temple in the name of Emperor Vespesians. Later, the temple became a good source of marble for the construction of other buildings.

POLLIO
FOUNTAIN

Across from the Temple of Domitian, the high arch of the Pollio Fountain scrapes the sky. The arch was supporting a triangular pediment. The semicircular brick wall was faced with marble reliefs. In front of the curved wall stood the statues of Odysseus and Polyphemus (exhibited in the Museum of Ephesus). This 1st Century B.C. construction is one of many fountains - each had a different flow of water to make a different decorative scene. The water in the Pollio Fountain was flowing slowly into the pool through the semicircular wall. The speed of the flow was slow so it could fill up the pool but not disturb the calmness of the water. The images of the statues were reflected on the surface of the pool.

The Temple of Domitian was decorated with a set of statues telling a Homerie Story:

"In the fields around Ephesus, if you were to put a stick in the ground and if the stick has even a little bit of life left to it then, it will sprout within a couple of weeks!"

THE MEMIUS MONUMENT

As the road curves down, on the right stands the Monument of Memius.
"Caius Memius, the savior, is the son of
Caius, grandson of Cornelius Sulla"
These lines were inscribed on the monument. All three mentioned in the inscriptions were illustrated in the reliefs depicting warriors and their trophies of war. Sulla, the Roman dictator, had saved Ephesus from enemy occupation. In memory of his victory, this four-sided, arch-shaped, victory monument was erected. One inscription shows this monument was restored by a Roman Emperor in the 3rd Century A.D. In spite of several restorations and with most of the blocks with figures missing, still the original construction can easily be visualized. The base was made of local stone and the monument, itself, was made of marble. On each facade, there were semicircular niches connected to each other by arches on which there were blocks with figures similar to caryatids.

The Domitian Square was the largest square in the city. The Temple of Domitian, the Pollio Fountain, the Hospital (?), and the Monument of Memius had surrounded the square on three sides. There was a colonnaded gallery on the other side. To complete the picture of the Domitian Square and to visualize the majestic look of the place, one should be able to build up the columns which lay on the ground. Scattered all around the Square one can see the big blocks of marble, which had carvings like teeth. The marble block which has the flying Nike figure is one of many blocks of stone used to decorate the street. So, if you can put all of these fragments together - the columns, topped with horizontal layers of marble, gracefully supporting "Nike" or similar figures-you can imagine what a joy for the eye it must have been to be in the Domitian Square long ago.

The Memius Monument,
the reliefs depicting varriors.

THE FOUNTAIN

To the side of the Monument of Memius stand four columns. Among so many striking constructions, these four columns might look too ordinary -until you can build the whole edifice in your imagination.

Instead of these four columns, try to imagine three sets of four columns on top of each other. A Corinthian capital can still be seen on one of the columns. There were similar capitals on all of them. The marble blocks which are laying on the side of the hill were placed horizontally on the capitals. There were four columns with capitals and decorative architraves, then another set of similar columns, and another set on top to make it look like a three-story high building. At the very top, there were three statues of women. The texture of the dress of these marble statues looked ordinary. They could have been wearing plain cotton dresses.

On the second floor there were three other female statues. The dresses of these women looked wet, sticking to their bodies. And, in the lowest part, there were statues of tritons and satyrs.

From underneath the feet of the women at the very top, water came tumbling down over the statues on the second floor and down into the narrow pool. Naturally, the dresses of the women on the second floor looked wet because of the water running over them. Though this picture alone is sufficient to make this fountain beautiful, the artistic genius who constructed this fountain used one more element to make it look even more impressive.

The sun rises early in the morning from behind the small hill in the back of the fountain. When an Ephesian walked into this section of the town from the narrow gate, he would be walking uphill, not able to see the sun itself but through thousands of drops of water dancing on the statues. He could see the colors of the sun split into thousands of particles of the seven colors. It would look like a fall of wonderful crystals.

The texture of the dresses is
ordinary cotton and
detinetely not wet.

The dresses are sticking
to the bodies of the statues,
to give a wet image.

THE GATE OF HERCULES

Certain animals were regarded as symbols of power. To transfer this power to the soul of a person, one had to wrap himself in the skin of such an animal (Diasporogmas). Hercules, here, is wearing the skin of the lion of Nemesis. The two identical reliefs on the gate, therefore, represent bravery, power, and determination.

These two pillars are the only things left of what was once a monumental two-story high gateway separating the residential part of the city from the state part. Facing the residential section of the town, it seems like Hercules, in his lion skin, wants to give a message. He might be saying, "If you want to go to the state part of the town with evil in your heart, you'll be killed just like this lion."

Ephesians, however, did not rely just on this message for the security they wanted. Either side of the gate was used to keep guards who would keep an eye on the ones who wanted to go through.

Giving your back to the Gate of Hercules, you should stop for a while and again use your imagination to visualize how much more beautiful the town must have been two thousand years before.

The valley which lies behind the white marble construction at the end of the road used to be part of the Aegean Sea. When there was even a little bit of breeze there would be white surf on the sea. Then, it had seemed like the white marble of the street continued into the sea on the white surf. With the deep blue color of the sky reflected in the sea, the sight looked like the best example of harmony between Nature's and Man's creations.

On either side of the street there were statues and behind the statues there were colonnaded sidewalks covered with a roof so people could walk under the sun or in the rain just as comfortably. Along the side of the sidewalk, there were shops. Though completely silted in, the entrances to these shops can still be seen. One can imagine the people, with their white togas flying in the air, rushing in and out of those shops.

In the street, on the marble pavement, there are lines and dots. These were put there to keep the horses from slipping.

There must have been chariots drawn by one or two horses running up and down the street. One can imagine the horses dashing down as they went downhill and moving very slowly as they came uphill. If you can, try to hear the squeaking of the wooden wheels over the marble pavement.

This street was named after the Curetes. In mythology, the Curetes were

The Curetes Street.

the semi-gods who clashed their arms, making a lot of noise so the jealous wife of Zeus would not hear the birth of Artemis and Apollo, the twins of Leto and Zeus. Later, the Curetes were identified with a class of priests in Ephesus. This group (of, at first six, later nine Curetes) were responsible for recreating the birth of Artemis. They worshipped her with cries and clashing cymbals and drums.

THE
FOUNTAIN OF
TRAJAN

Emperor Trajan had been to all of the Roman Provinces. Wherever he went, there was a colossal construction built in his name. Some were large, impressive temples, some were big palaces... but, in this great city of Ephesus, he had preferred to have a building of modest scale. But with an important message.

Before explaining how and why the fountain was important in meaning, let's try to visualize what it had looked like. The fountain was "U"-shaped, two-stories high, with a pool in the center. If one can replace in his imagination the cement blocks of the restoration with the marble column standing next to the fountain, he can get a better idea of the size of it. Between the columns there stood the statues of the gods, legendary heroes (Androklos), and members of the royal family. The statue of the Emperor Trajan, about three times normal human size, stood in the center. Today, only a globular figure and a foot of his statue can be seen.

The importance of the fountain comes from this statue, which was built during the reign of the Emperor (98-117 A.D.).

This guidebook has tried to avoid emphasis on dates and names as much as possible to give the verbal images of the site rather than the easy to forget information. However, the date here is very important. The fountain was built early in the 2nd Century A.D.

In this statue, Trajan was stepping on a globular figure. The quotation underneath read, "I conquered it all, it's all under my foot."

He meant the world was under his foot. Since the world was stylized in a globular figure, he must have known the world is round. He had preferred to leave this message at no other place, where colossal buildings were erected in his name, but here in Ephesus. The reason why he chose Ephesus to leave such a revolutionary message is because he trusted the Ephesians, who were raised up by the teachings of their native philosopher, Herakleitos.

Herakleitos had stated his philosophy in these words, "No one can wash his feet twice in the same water because everything is changing, everything is turning." He was trying to teach people tolerance for a changing world. He was saying new things might come up in one's life. One should not necessarily believe but one should at least respect the new ideas. In the early 2nd Century A.D., maybe the Ephesians did not believe the world is round but at least they allowed this message to be left here.

The Fountain of Trajan.

In front of the fountain there is a waterway. When they needed to wash the Curetes Street, they would overflow the water out from the pool of the fountain. Over the grooved surface of the marble the water would cascade onto the street.

SCHOLASTIKIA
BATH

Turning right on the side street which intersects the Curetes Street, you will find one of the two entrances of this three storied construction. The public baths used to be regarded as more of a social building than just a place to take a bath. Therefore the structure of the bath was arranged to serve the function of the building.

The bathers would undress in the apoditerium. The sudotorium was warm enough to make one sweat. There, lying on the couchs, they would relax, sweat, and adjust their bodies to the heat of the next and hottest room, the caldarium. After washing and having a nice massage in the caldarium, the next stop was the tepidarium. Here, not only did they cool off but, in the relaxing atmosphere of this tepid room, they enjoyed discussing politics, philosophy and daily affairs. Swimming in the cool water pool in the last room, the frigidarium, was a rejuvenating finale to the very popular public "ritual".

Walking down the four steps from the side street, you will find yourself in the apoditerium. The marble floors and the marble-faced walls were all spotless white, as if symbolizing the "purification ritual" which was to start there and last for several hours. The statue of the lady, Scholastikia, is one of the many statues which decorated the large hall. Scholastikia, who had restored the bath in 400, is sitting in her chair with a straight back and a very dignified posture... as if she wants to say that then the women had the right to own property and run a business in the middle of the town.

The next room is the frigidarium. The oval-shaped cold water pool was a place where, for many centuries, many men and women must have enjoyed dipping . The entrance of the tepidarium is through the arched gate. The terra-cotta pipes lain under the floor and in the walls were used to circulate hot air. The narrow door gives an access to the caldarium. The floor was built on brick columns. Brick can retain heat for a long time. The furnace (hipocaust) was behind the arches to the left of the floor. Hot air coming out from the furnace circulated through the brick columns. The heated bricks kept the floor warm. A very low price was charged for the baths. The poor could use the facilities as much as the rich but, it was sort of an unspoken agreement between the poor and the rich to use this public building at different times of the day.

The rich came in during the afternoon after the Forum and the Basilica closed down. Slaves or servants helped their masters wash in the caldarium. The heavy smell of the herbs and oil used to massage the masters made this large room smell like a flower shop.

The Scholastikia Bath.

In the 1st Century A.D., men and women bathed in the same building, at different hours. Later, they could use the bath at the same time.

Several times through history the restoration of the bath was made by use of the marble brought from the town hall.

THE MOSAIC-PAVED SIDEWALK

Back on the Curetes Street... across from the Scholastikia Bath lies the multi-colored, very nicely preserved, mosaic sidewalk. There were marble benches scattered on the mosaics. This is a very artistic example of the most common Mediterranean taste of public life style, sidewalk cafes, restaurants, benches are what the Mediterranean people can not do without.

The Ephesians did not build their city to make it into a masterpiece of art. They built it as beautiful as it is by using many works of art, such as: decorative marble carvings, statues, and very time consuming and talent demanding mosaic works. They did this because they took pride in the site where they were living. Harmony without monotony is what they achieved through their architecture and decoration.

THE NARROW STREET

The narrow street which starts by the mosaic climbs up to another street which runs parallel to the Curetes Street. Going up the steps not too far from the main road, there is a drainage with several holes. Before the road intersects with the other road, on the pavement there are two illustrations, a fish and two overlapping crosses with a circle around them. The Christians in the early times of Christianity were frightened of persecution but they would still leave a mark to show that Christians lived in that locality. The fish was the symbol for Jesus. In ancient Greek the word for fish is ΙΧΘΥΣ. The letters of this word stand for the first letters of the following words:

´Ι, stands for ΙΧΣΟΥΣ which is Jesus.
´Χ, stands for ΧΡΗΣΤΟΣ which is Christ.
´Θ, stands for ΘΕΟΣ which is God.
´Υ, stands for ΥΙΟΣ which is Son.
´Σ, stands for ΣΩΤΗΡ which is Saviour.

In other words, the Fish, ΙΧΘΥΣ, is Jesus Christ, the Son of God, the Saviour. If you put the letters of ΙΧΘΥΖ in the form of a symbol you get...

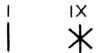

If the ends of these lines are closed, the result is the Maltese cross....

So, the Maltese cross actually stands for Jesus Christ, the Son of God, the Saviour. On the marble pavements of the main streets and on the steps of the state agora there are quite a few of these symbols.

Ephesus was a very important trade and religious center. Being the capitol of the province of Asia had given Ephesus considerable political importance, as well. The population of this metropole, therefore, was around 250.000 people for more than three hundred years after the 1st Century A.D. The poor and the members of the lower classes lived outside the city. Landowners, merchants, sailors, laborers, craftsmen, and the priests made up the upper class and they were settled not too far away from the center of the city. However, the Roman citizens, who were few in number, were the leaders of the city. This privileged group of people could afford to live in the very center of Ephesus. The location of their houses was chosen to be close to all major public buildings like the library, the baths, and the agora.

For the construction of the houses of the poor, cobblestone and mortar made of clay and straw were used. They did not have bathrooms or toilets. Since most of these houses were built outside the city and on the hillside at a level higher than the city water reservoir, they did not have running water, either. The houses of the rich stand as a total contrast to those of the less fortunate.

The water drained into the perfect sewer system of the city through the drains on the pavement.

The Fish.

To make the houses of the upper class comfortable, beautiful, and solid no effort or expense was spared.

Home was considered sacred. It was like a small shrine. The family traditions and manners in the house always had a spiritual attribution. Goddess Vesta, the goddess of the hearth, was the protectress of the house. Her statuette was kept in a niche. Food, wine, and various other small gifts were offered to her to keep the evil away from the house and to ensure prosperity.

This is still a living tradition in Anatolia. If one walks in a Turkish house, it is very common to see a bundle of wheat, blue eye, a mirror, and an empty egg shell hanging over the door.

Walking into the house, you would come down to a vestibule. The proper thing to do was to walk in with the right foot first. There is a fountain in the vestibule.

The purpose for this once tile-faced fountain is very obvious. Before entering the house, the 'shrine', one had to cleanse himself. Walking straight ahead, there is the courtyard, the peristyle of the house. The top of the marble-paved section was open. It was the main source of light for the house. Naturally, with no roof, the rain fell in, too. The word 'impluvium', meaning rain hall, was also used to name such courtyards. The floor around the impluvium was completely surrounded with the fine work of mosaics. The yellow and black stones were laid in such an artistic manner that no one can doubt the talent of the Ephesian workers.

The frescoes on the walls showed there was no limit what an artist could

create to decorate the walls. The figures varied from a workman preparing mortar to romantic floral designs.

The large room which opens up to the peristyle is called the theater room. The frescoes reflected the tastes and the occupation of the owners of the houses. Through the centuries, as the owners were changed, according to the interests and occupation of each new owner, the frescoes were either replaced or painted over by different frescoes.

In this room it is easy to see the frescoes of different periods. The frescoes of the upper and lower levels vary in characer and theme. To the left of the door, on the main panel, a scene from Euripides' play 'Orestes' is portrayed

using the main characters, Orestes and his sister, Electra. Scenes from other popular plays were depicted on the other panels.

The fresco on one of the panels is an illustration of an adventure of Hercules. Hercules fought the river-god, Achelous, because Achelous was in love with the girl Hercules wanted to marry. Knowing his power, Achelous had no desire to fight him and he tried to reason with Hercules. But that did not work with Hercules. It only made him angrier. He said, "My hand is better than my tongue, let me win fighting, and you may win talking." Achelous took the form of a bull and attacked Hercules fiercely but the hero was used to handling bulls. He conquered the river-god and broke off one of his horns. The main cause of the contest, a young princess named Deianira, became his wife.

The who had once lived in the Houses of Ephesus!

SERVICE
AREA

To the right of the vestibule there is a service area which is well preserved to show the heating system of the houses. As it was in the Scholastikia Bath, the heating system in the house was through circulating hot air under the floor and through the earthen pipes inlaid in the walls.

THE SECOND HOUSE

It was a large house with many rooms and a second floor. On the left corner of the peristyle there is a stairway leading up to the second floor. Not only the mosaics on the floors but the glass mosaic on the ceiling is breathtaking in this house.

The biggest room, with two fountains on the wall, was the dining hall. Meals were eaten in a religious atmosphere. The burning incense and the wine sprinkled on the floor of the dining room completed the picture of this very ritualistic eating cereony. The running water system was well laid in but it was not always reliable. Every house, therefore, made sure there was a well in the impluvium.

The furniture was either of marble or of bronze. The decor of the rooms were completed with small statuettes... some of which are displayed in the museum.

THE
TEMPLE OF
HADRIAN

This Roman Emperor, who had edifices built in his name on three continents - from England to North Africa, spent only a few months in Ephesus. Within the very short time he was there, this temple was built and dedicated in his name (138 A.D.). The marble had to be quarried out and brought here. Engineers, architects, masons, workers, and artists had to work very hard and fast to get this temple completed within the few months.

It is not the size but the decoration which makes the temple one of the most attractive edifices in Ephesus.

In front of the facade, there are four columns supporting a triangular frontal. All you can now see of this triangular frontal is the supporting arch, which has the bust of the goddess of the city, Tyche, on the keystone.

On either side of the gate, on the walls, there is a row of frieze depicting gods, goddesses, Dionysiac procession, and legends. On the right side, the figures standing side by side are Athena, Selene (the goddess of the moon), a man, Apollo, a female figure, Androcules Heracles, Emperor Theodosius, and Athena.

The figures on the left, adjacent to the gate, are four female figures holding arms and shields. They are the Amazons. According to one theory, it was the Amazons who were to settle in Ephesus first. On the other side, however, there is another illustration about the foundation of the town. Androcules, the legendary founder of the city, is chasing the boar who was scared of the fire that was started by the fish. (The legend was told in the beginning of this book.) So, both legends about the foundation of Ephesus were illustrated in the friezes.

On the inner arch, above the gate, there is a relief of a woman. She is believed to be Medusa. She was always represented by just her head but here we can see the goddess with a full body. Most probably, this was a relief of another woman but, after the work was completed, the artist must have walked back and looked at his work. He must have thought, 'This beautiful temple... a gorgeous work of art needs a protection." Then he must have changed the head of that woman, whoever she was, into Medusa to ward off the evil eye.

Warding off evil is what we still very strongly believe in Anatolia. The blue eye figures swinging on the windows of buses, the small blue charms pinned on the shoulders of the little ones, the large, decorative blue hanging on the doors of the houses and shops... are all examples of this living paganistic tradition. It was the power of the look in Medusa's eyes which warded off the evil. After we accepted the monotheistic religions we could not have gone

The Temple of Hadrian.

around carrying the head of a goddess of the paganistic world. The traditions were very difficult to change, though. So, a compromise - no more goddesses to ward off the evil, but an eye is sufficient to do the same thing without offending the religious belief too much. In fact, among the Christians of this region, the blue eye is transformed into a blue-eyed fish (IXΘΥΣ - Jesus) to double up the power of the blue eye.

This is a very important fact of this part of the world, the names of the religions change, the empires come, the empires go, but the traditions and cultures are so deep rooted that there is always a living sign of a tradition which might be thousands of years old.

Half-way down the wall, there is a line of reliefs which look like running swastika with squares in between. This figure is called the 'key figure'. The lines represent the meandering rivers. The squares are the fields in between the meanders of the rivers. The flowers in the squares stand for fertility of the

fields. For a community where most of the people made their living off agriculture, what else would have been the 'key' to their happiness more than the fertile fields in between the meandering rivers? This figure has been used to decorate the works of art created by people for ages. What used to decorate the architectural beauty then is now decorating the Anatolian handcrafts of this region - the carpets. On the handmade carpets of western Anatolia it is alway possible to trace this pattern of meandering rivers.

Athena, Selena, Apollo.
From the Temple of Hadrian.

THE
PUBLIC
TOILETS

This is a very social public toilet. There was no separation between the seats. The Ephesians must have enjoyed using the toilet together. Even in the houses the private facility had three seats. They cared a lot about the way this toilet was decorated. The walls were all faced with marble, the mosaics on the floors were just as exquisite as the ones in the houses. There was a pool in the center. It was surrounded by marble columns and there were marble statues of dolphins with Eros riding on them. Through the hollow mouths of the dolphins the water flowed into the pool.

There was a man playing music in one corner. They did not need the music for its aesthetic value but to compete with the sounds of forty-eight people using the toilet at the same time.

They used to love chatting there. Probably most of the gossip in the town originated from this public toilet.

The marks in the entrance show there must have been a door. When so many people were seated in the toilet side by side they obviously did not care for privacy. Then, why did they need a door? It was put there so the caretakers of the toilet could control the ones who came in... because there was a charge for the toilet. The people who refused to pay used the corners of the streets. This was subject to a severe punishment. In fact, there was a plaque on the wall of the commercial agora which read, "He who pisses on this spot will be hounded down by the vengeance of the three-headed gods."

The pod in the puplic toilet.

THE OCTAGON- THE BYZANTINE FOUNTAIN

Though the Ephesians were able to create almost an eternal city, they themselves were nothing more than mortals.They died of natural causes, they were massacred, the earthquakes, epidemics of plague and malaria took the lives of thousands and thousands of Ephesians.

They had their own burial traditions. Their necropole, or cemetery, was outside the city walls. According to their income level, some were buried in sarchophages, some were simply laid in the ground, some had a room or two built for the whole family.

It was strongly believed that there was life after death. Personal belongings, gifts, food, wine, and candles were left in the graves. Those who broke into the graves were punished. They were made to pay high fines to the city treasury.

During the funeral ceremony, the relatives of the deceased walked by the corpse and called out his name for the last time. A group of people was hired to do the crying.

Only those people who were very popular among the Ephesians were allowed to be buried in the city.The most common reasons for being granted this privilege were for organizing competitions, donating money to the temples, or financial support for the upkeep of the official buildings.

In the lower end of the Curetes Street, there are two examples of such burials.

The Octagon, the octagonal mausoleum, was dedicated to a young woman. It was built on a rectangular base which was three steps above the street level. Eight Corinthian columns were supporting an octagonal roof.

Next to the Octagon, there is a row of tablets which are before the other mausoleum. The inscriptions on these tablets were the degrees of the emperors, laws and regulations concerning the city. The restoration of the city and the city wall after the earthquake in the Fourth Century A.D., the holidays in the Asian province, the fines to be imposed on those who would pollute the streets and the harbour... these were a few of those important notes put on this public 'bulletin stone'.

The fountain, which is decorated with crosses and other wall decorations of Byzantine character, was built as a mausoleum originally. Later in the Byzantine period, it was rearranged into a pool. Being right in the center of the town, it was a very popular place among those who wanted to pass the time during the day.

The city created by the Ephesians
might be eternal,
but the Ephesians themselves were mortals,
they died too....

THE END OF CURETES STREET

If you turn around, you'll get the feeling of the beautiful street which winds up to the sky.

In the middle of the street there is an iron ring. This was a manhole. If something went wrong with the sewer system they would go through the hole and repair it. During the excavations, quite a number of coins, statuettes, and other items were found in the pipes. Obviously, they were dropped in the sewer system from the houses and passed into the main channel. This shows that the city had a very good working network for their sewer system. When the pipes were clogged pieces were cut out of the upper part of the pipes and mended by terra-cotta after the blocking item was removed.

Before you turn right from Curetes Street, on the left there was a Monumental Gate located in front of a side street. Four pairs of columns were supporting a marble-faced wall. There were six pairs of smaller columns at the top floor. Having this monumental gate in the entrance of the side street suggests that the street probably leads to a sacred location which has not been excavated yet.

A Chariot.

The iron ring at the end of
the Curetes Street shows
where the man hole is.

THE LIBRARY OF CELCUS

On either side of the Marble Road, there are two public buildings. The one which stands up with dignity and glamour is the Library of Celcus.

Tiberius Celcus (60-114 A.D.) was the proconsul, the governor of the Asian Province. Before he was given this job, in Rome he was in charge of all the public buildings. When he died, his son wanted his father's burial ground to reflect what Celcus had spent his life doing. A charming architectural masterpiece, open for public use, a library, was the most appropriate monumental tomb.

The sarcophagus of Celcus is located under the main floor of the library. Finely decorated, the marble sarcophagus has a very modest look compared to the rest of the construction. It seems as though, once more, the underlying objective of the construction was its public use rather than its being used as a monumental tomb.

The interior of the Library was a rather wide place (10.92m × 16.72m), divided into three floors by two galleries. Opposite the main entranceway, in the central niche, was the statue of goddess Pallas Athena, leading the way to enlightenment. The daylight poured into the library through the large windows.

The facade of the library was carefully planned to make it appear colossal within the rather narrow space the building had to fit. The nine steps carried the eye upward to the colonnaded gallery in front of the main entrance. The pairs of columns were spaced differently so the ones in the center were farther apart from each other than the ones on the outer sides. By using this method, the architect wanted to give the building a perspective which would disillusion the eye for the width of the facade, making it appear wider than it actually is.

The second set of columns, setting on the protruding beams, was framing the windows of the upper floor. These columns were smaller than the lower ones. The effect they wanted to achieve by using the different sizes was to give a feeling of weightlessness to create an image of ascending to heaven.

ΣΟΦΙΑ
ΚΕΛΣΟΥ

a feeling of
weightlessness to create an
image of ascending to heaven.

At the very top, on the triangular and semicircular frontals, the face of Medusa is loyally doing her job, warding off the evil eye.

Not only were they able to build a beautiful building but they were also able to apply an ingenious technique of architecture. They built double walls around the building. Air was ventilated through the walls so humidity and insects would not deteriorate the valuable scrolls of parchment or papyrus. There were around 12.000 scrolls.

Through the pair of columns once can see the statues of four women. They

stand for the virtues admired most: knowledge, friendship, understanding, and wisdom.

During the Third Century, the library was destroyed by the Goths; later, earthquakes and other natural causes over the centuries swallowed the glamour of the library. By the Fourth Century, the library was no longer in use as a library. But the Ephesians found another use for the facade of this once very popular public building. They built a fountain in the middle of the steps. A pool was built in the courtyard. Either side of the pool and the steps of the road leading down to the courtyard were used as an auditorium. It must have been a very motivating location for the lecturers to give their lectures. They would have been speaking to their audience from the steps of the library while the listeners encircled the pool, which was reflecting the image of the enchanting facade.

The statues symbolizing
the virtues admired most...
Knowledge, Friendship, Understanding, Wisdom.

THE MAZEUS-MITHRIDATES GATE

The monumental gate next to the library was dedicated to a Roman emperor, Augustus, his wife, Livia, and his children.

The gate is a choice example of how contrasting values can be portrayed side by side.

The inscriptions on the wall use very sophisticated language, "Emperor Caesar, Augustus, son of gods, the high priest, twelve times consul, twenty times tribune, and Livia, wife of Caesar Augustus, Marc Agrippa, son of Lucius, three times consul, emperor, six times tribune, and daughter of Julio Caesar Augustus, from Mazeus and Mithridates to their masters and to the people."

The inscription inside the gate, however, was very simple and straight forward. It read, "One who pisses here will be tried in the court."

Utmost care and attention was given to make the gate look majestic. Bronze was embedded in the inscriptions to make them look striking but all this effort was not good enough not to make a spelling mistake... writing 'Imperatori' for Emperor, 'Imp' was spelled 'Imb'.

Mazeus and Mithridates, who had the gate built, were once slaves. Though slavery contradicts with wealth, this monument is a good example of what emancipated slaves could achieve. They could get rich enough to adorn their town with such a big and expensive monument.

The Mazeus - Mithridates gate
built by two emancipated slaves.

THE
LOVE HOUSE

The dignified ladies of the library who stand for the virtues of knowledge, understanding, friendship, and wisdom are facing another public building on the other side of the road, the love house.

To get in the building with clean feet was a must. There is a narrow passage from the Marble Road to the main entrance of the house. On the corner just before the gate was a marble-paved basin filled with water. It was used to wash off the dust and dirt from the feet. The bust of the patroness was sitting on the small, graceful pillar in the basin. The two-story high brothel had private rooms upstairs. To keep the privacy there were no windows. Candles were sufficient to light the rooms, which were flooded with the erotic scent of the incense burned. The candles and the incense burners were placed in the notches in the walls.

The first floor was more of a socializing area, with halls and a good-sized dining room. The floors were marble-paved or covered with mosaics. In the main hall, the floor mosaic has portraits of four women. Some interpret these four different women as symbols for the four seasons, indicating that the house was open year-round.

There was not too much furniture. Divans, sofas, and tables were stone and built-in with the building.

The convivial hours were best assured with the wine served to the visitors. The ladies working here were good at making this aphrodisiac wine, as well. In fact, they would do it in the living quarters. The wine press and the wine vault is still next to the mosaic-paved room.

In the room next to the Curetes Street, there is a well which is still being used. On a hot summer day, even today, the well is a life saver with its pure, cold water. It almost feels divine when you desperately need to cool off while walking in the marble streets of Ephesus under the bright, hot sun. But the well, then, had a more important reason to be there. It was believed to be sacred and, supposedly, a cup of the water would help women to have babies. The sterile women, who had their dreams of having a baby come true, showed their gratitude by throwing offerings into the well. Valuable personal belongings and various statuettes were found in this well. The most popular offering was the statue of Priapus, god for the cause of fertility.

One of the social buildings on the Marble Road
was the brothel...

THE
MARBLE
ROAD

The road which starts in front of the Celcus Library and the Brothel stretches toward the theater. Though almost everything else in Ephesus is made of marble, when a visitor turns around the corner to walk this marble way (where even the sidewalks are made of marble) the immediate reaction is to ask 'where does all this marble come from?' The marble quarries were not too far away, most of it came from within twenty to thirty miles. But it was still quite a job to get these huge blocks down into the town.

Walking along the street, the visitors usually notice one other curious thing along the wall on the side of the road. The notches remain where the iron and lead clamps were used to hold the blocks of marble together. During the Byzantine period, these were removed and melted into coins or weapons.

For those of you who might be wondering how much more of the city is laying underground, the answer is visible. A few yards past the site of the library, if you turn around, on your left, you would see that only less than a quarter of the hill has been excavated. On the right, next to the houses on the hill, almost no work has been done - in spite of continuous work for more than a hundred years. If you consider that these proportions are around the city where most of the excavations have been made, it is not difficult to appreciate the prediction of the archeologist who estimates hundreds of years will pass before everything is excavated in Ephesus.

To the left of the road, on the two-meter high wall, there was a colonnaded walkway covered with a roof. The columns on the street side were topped with marble blocks. These very decorative pieces were used not only to make the road more beautiful but they served a very important purpose, as well. There was a waterway running at the very top. Lion faces, with their hollow mouths, were facing down the street. When it got unbearably hot in the street they would let water run in the waterway from one end of the street to the other. The water dropped onto the street through the hollow mouths of the lions. The Ephesians cleaned and cooled their street in the most aesthetic manner.

On the sidewalk, on the left, halfway up the street, a graffiti representing a heart, a left foot, a woman's head, and a rectangular figure catches the visitor's eye. This was an advertisement especially designed for the men coming from the harbour. The heart is slightly farther away from the rest of the illustrations and it has dots on it, showing a broken, lonely heart. The writing in the rectangular figure was a tariff. In other words, the message of the graffiti was, "If your heart is lonely and a bit broken, then the way to the brothel is on the left foot side. If you want a nice looking woman like this one, you'd better have your money in your pocket."

Somebody who was curious about the price had calculated it and put the inflation rate on it and said that the price had not changed too much.

Walking on the white marble streets, one can not help but adore the beauty of this city. But, actually, it is not the marble which makes this city as beautiful as it is. It is the engineering that was involved in the construction of the whole town. Ingenious engineering techniques can be seen farther down the road where one of the marble blocks has been removed from the pavement. The hole is exposing the sub-structure of the street. There are two arches, not even a yard apart from each other. There were hundreds of these arches in the center of the street and there are hundreds more on the side. If you look at the terrain around the street, it is quite rugged. But the Marble Road stretches very straight. The center of the Road is higher than the sides. The slight slope down toward the sides was made intentionally to get proper drainage. They achieved this perfect construction by those arches.

Along the sides of the Marble Road there are blocks with reliefs of gladiators. One composition is depicting a gladiator facing a feather. The feather is representing a pen. The gladiator, in full armament, is fighting with the feather. The feather is standing straight and proud like a victor. It seems this is a two thousand - year old interpretation of "the pen is mightier than the sword."

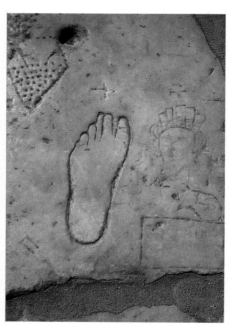

The water dropped
on to the Marble Road
through the mouths
of the lions....

If your heart is
feeling lonely, the way
to the brothel is
on the left foot side...
A popular advertisement!

THE COMMERCIAL AGORA

Starting from the 3rd Century B.C., Ephesians continued to grow into the most prosperous commercial center of Western Anatolia and controlled all the area's banking affairs. Its world-famous harbour was a wide-open gate for foreign merchandise. Its rich and fertile fields around the city were an endless source of agricultural products. The city of Ephesus also attracted many people because of its distinguished, celebrated craftsmen. The Commercial Agora was where the majority of this economic activity of the town was centered.

It was a square area, completely paved with marble and surrounded on all sides by colonnaded galleries and shops. The life in the agora started very early in the morning. The voices of the dealers trying to sell the glasswork, luxury fabrics, incense, spices, papyrus brought from Syria, the Orient, India, Arabia, and Egypt could be heard in one corner of the agora. The artists, silversmiths, sculptors, and painters worked quietly at another corner.

Visiting the agora, even if not for shopping, was part of the routine of daily life. Some would enjoy chatting with their friends, some would buy a new slave, and some would make vital decisions about investing all their wealth into the money dealers sitting behind the low benches.

As the agora went through different phases of development, it was made more beautiful and functionally more efficient by new additions. There were statues, dedicatory inscriptions decorating the porticos, wells to keep the fish, fruit, etc., cool.

This huge complex needed good supervision. An agoranome was the head of a group of people working hard controlling the prices, the quality, and so on. They made sure the scales were weighing correctly.

The sundial and the water clock found in the center of the agora suggests they were time consicous. The market had to open and close down at a certain time.

The rock building on
the top of the hill
is where St. Paul was
kept after the riot
in the theater.

THE
THEATER

Could it be the size which impresses every visitor? Maybe it is the perfect construction which proudly resisted the 2200 years, as if saying, "I was once built for Dionysiac festivals but I will welcome the orchestras which play the concertos of Tchaikovsky as well." The immortality of its grandeur can be lived by just sitting on the seats. One can hear Oedipus stating Sophocles play "Child of a blind man, Antigone" The fury of the mad Ephesians shouting "Great is Artemis of the Ephesians" can still shake the visitor if he wants to think of the excitement that St.Paul went through here when Demetrius started the riot.

It feels as though the political conversations of the council meetings or the cymbals of the dancers will be heard any minute.

The theater was built in the Second Century B.C. but went through several restorations throughout the centuries. The most important thing about the theater is the role it played in the history of Christianity. The best way to understand how it had happened is to go through the days of St.Paul in Ephesus:

St.Paul had visited Ephesus twice. His first brief visit was at the end of his second missionary journey on his way from Corinth to Antioch. His second stay lasted for a period of two years during which time the Christian church was either established or strengthened. Finally, at the end of his third missionary journey, he met once more with the elders of the Ephesian Church in the port of Miletus.

During his first stay, St.Paul visited the local synagogue. The curiosity of those assembled was aroused but his ship had to depart for Syria. Before St.Paul left Ephesus, his disciples told the Apostle that they would very much like to see him back in Ephesus. They told him that not only were there 250.000 people living in the city but there were many others coming to Ephesus from various places for trade and religious purposes so if he were able to pass unto them the word of God then they could go back to their towns and do the same. So, the people in the most remote parts of Anatolia where St.Paul could never find time to go in his lifetime could hear the word of God. St. Paul was persuaded. He promised that he'd be back. He left Ephesus, leaving Aquila and Priscilla behind.

St.Paul kept his promise and returned to Ephesus.

The only place where he could preach was the synagogue but, after three months of preaching, St.Paul was evicted from the synagogue. Tyrannus, an Ephesian teacher, offered his hall. St. Paul transferred his preaching to the hall of Tyrannus. There, not only was he trying to pass the word of God unto

The theater.
The perfect construction which proudly
resisted 2200 years.

the Ephesians, but he was also creating miracles in the name of God. He was blessing the aprons and handkerchiefs of the ill ones and he was getting those people well. His reputation was growing bigger in the city every day. St. Paul's success in preaching and the reverence with which he was regarded by converts, gave Jewish exorcists the idea that they could steal his power by using the same words that Paul used. They wanted to prove to the people of Ephesus that Paul's method was not an extraordinary thing. When, one day, a well-know Ephesian was possessed by an evil spirit, his family asked the most trustworthy exorcist to get rid of the evil spirit. Thinking that this would be the perfect opportunity to prove that he could be just like Paul, the exorcist went to the house of the possesed man. He moved by the bed. He raised up his hand, just like Paul would have done and he said, "In the name of God and Jesus Christ, I ask you to leave the body", of this man just like Paul would have said. But the possessed man got up on his feet and shouted at the exorcist saying, "I know God, I know Jesus Christ, but I don't know you; who are you?" The exorcist was kicked out from the house in front of many Ephesians who came there to see the outcome of this new method. Soon, they found out that their trustworthy exorcist was not as powerful as St.Paul and they rushed up

to the house of the Governor. They told the governor that they wanted to listen to Paul. Just for this once, the governor allowed Paul to give a speech publicly. Actually, the governor had no other choice but give this permission because whether he allowed it or not, he realized, the people were determined to listen to him anyway. The word went around the town fast and soon the Ephesians started pouring into the theater. There were thirty-five thousand people squeezed in the theater, anxiously waiting for the lecture of this man who was talking about a God that they had never seen or touched before. Just before the Apostle came into the theater, a craftsman named Demetrius came running down the steps. He stood in the center of the orchestra and with a very persuasive tone he started talking to the Ephesians. Demetrius was saying, "If you let this man talk to you, half of you will be Christians immediately, and in not more than two years time, half of Anatolia will be christians. Do you know what he says?", Demetrius asked the question. The Ephesians were very confused, they did not know what to answer. Demetrius carried on saying, "If you believe in the words of his God, then you'd believe that there should be no manmade gods. If everybody believes in that then, to whom are we going to sell the silver shrines of Artemis, who will come to show respect to our Mother in her temple..." What Demetrius was really asking was that if they

were to believe in Paul, how were they going to make their living. The Ephesians immediately realized what sort of threat St.Paul was for them and they started a riot. For two hours, thirty-five thousand people in one voice cried out the same word, Great is Artemis of Ephesus, Great is Artemis of Ephesus... Their voices were carried out into the streets. The ones who did not know what was going on in the theater, hearing the voices, realized that there was something wrong. Some people were running up the marble streets, some running down. One was shouting one thing and another was shouting another. There was an absolute chaos in the streets.

St. Paul was insisting that he would not leave the town. He was sure that his turn would come and he would be able to speak to the Ephesians. The Ephesians in the theater were getting ready to go out and kill the Apostle. Just at that second, the city clerk came into the theater and stopped the shouting. He must have realized that this was no simple riot. They were too mad to know what they were doing. After they killed St.Paul and his friends they could go around killing all the other Roman citizens, forgetting why they had started the riot. To save his and his Roman friends lives in this city, the city clerk told them that, unless they went away peacefully, the Roman authorities might look upon the incident as a riot against the Romans and impose the usual penalties, which were very high fines. The Ephesians loved

Christianity had flourished
in Ephesus with the
arrival of St. Paul.

the money only when it was in their own pockets so they decided not to kill Paul but get rid of him in a different way. St. Paul was taken to the rock building at the top of the hill, at the end of the city walls and he was shipped to Alexandria of Troas and from there to Kavala in Mesodonia.

The messages which St.Paul wanted to give in the theater of Ephesus were then written in the letters of St. Paul to The Ephesians. These messages can be read in the Bible under the headline of "The Epistle of Apostle Paul to the Ephesians" Who knows, maybe if Paul were allowed to talk to The Ephesians in this Theater, he would not have written the letters to the Ephesians and the Bible would have had one chapter less...

THE ARCADIAN AVENUE (THE HARBOUR STREET)

The wide street which connects the theater to the harbour is called the Arcadian Avenue. From the foot of the steps, the street had extended for six hundred yards. At the end was the sea. At the end of the street where you can see one column higher than the others, there were four big columns which were like the entrance to the harbour. Sitting in the steps, in the shade of the olive tree, please try to pretend you are a spectator in the theater two thousand years ago. The performance in the theater would be over just before the sun set. You would leave the theater by walking down the steep steps. As you walked down the steps, you would see the sun setting behind the "Hill of St.Paul". The crimson red sky would reflect in the sea. The sail boats would be sailing in or out the harbour. A short man with a torch in his hand would be reaching up to light the torches which were sticking out from the columns on either side of the street. He would light the torches one by one. As the sun went further down behind the hill the brighter the street would get in front of you with the lit torches and you would slowly walk down and join the rest for an evening promenade.

... as the sun went
further down behind the hill
the brighter the street
would get with the lit torches.

THE
THEATER
GYMNASIUM

To the right of the theater where the Arcadiana Avenue intersects the road which stretches towards the Temple of Artemis, the remains of the largest gymnasium of the city can be seen. By late antiquity, gymnasiums had fallen out of use, perhaps because the financial burden of providing oil was too great for the cities to bear, or because of changing fashions. But, since this gymnasium was built in a combination of a bath and an education center, it continued to function much longer than the others. Some restorations can be dated to as late as the 7th century A.D.

Where the gymnasium was a popular place to get both physical and academic training, the theater gymnasium was basicly used to train those who were to perform in the theater. Obviously, the training of the youth and actors was much of public concern because the seats at the paleastra, where various sports were practiced, outnumbers the number of students who would be trained at one time at the gymnasium.

The school complex had a library, five class rooms, conference rooms and a typical roman period bath with a tepidarium, frigidarium and a calderium.

THE BASILICA OF ST. MARY (THE COUNCIL CHURCH)

In the middle of the fourth century the former market place was converted to a very different function; a great church a three-aisled, apsed basilica with a narthex and large atrium. The floors were paved with marble and mosaic of geometric design and the walls were faced with marble. Columns of varying heights were reused, bases and capitals rarely matched. The atrium gave an access to a large domed octagonal baptistry. This great basilica was the cathedral of Ephesus, the Church of the Virgin Mary in which the Councils of 431 and 449 were held. In 431, the nature of the Holy Trinity was under discussion. The protagonists were Nestorius, Patriarch of Constantinople and Memnon of Ephesus. The latter was the victorious. The people of Ephesus were put to good use in the holy disputations. Rioters filled the Agora, surrounded the house where Nestorius was staying. "The people of Ephesus waited outside the church from dawn to dark, and gave a shout of joy when they heard the news that Nestorius has been deposed. When Cyril and Memnon emerged from the church of St. Mary, they were guided to their houses in a triumphal procession with lamps, preceded by women with censers of incense, in celebration, lamps were lit all over the city." (Clive Foss) It was agreed that Jesus was the Son of God, and thus divine motherhood of Virgin MARY was confirmed.

The divine motherhood of Mary
was accepted this Church.

THE STADIUM

The entrance to the stadium was through the monumental arch gate which can still be seen from a long distance away. One side of the stadium rests on a natural slope and the other was built on vaulted galleries. Being 230 meters lond and 30 meters wide, it is considered rather big stadium which could possibly seat 25000 people.

The stadium dates back to the Hellenistic Period. Like most every thing else in Ephesus, the stadium too was renovated during the Roman Period. During the reign of Emperor Nepro the seating places were reinforced and the whole building was addorned with statues and friezes.

The sports events of the Hellenistic and Early Roman period had been replaced by the horrible sights of Christian persecutions in the stadium. Once Christianity was established as the state religion, and once the christians had no more fears of the pegans, to get revenge of those days when religious tollerence was not even considered and in the name of one god, beleivers of an other God were killed; the Christians tore apart most of the stadium and used the works of art such as statues and other decorative carvings as ordinary construction materials.

Today camel fights are held in the stadium. With thousands of people sitting in the stadium to watch the camel fights, is seems like the 2300 year old building was built to last and to serve the interest of the people forever.

The Gladiators.

THE
MUSEUM

The artifacts displayed in the first room were found in the houses of Ephesus. Most of them date to the First through the Third Centuries A.D. Next to the entrance, on the wall, there are three frescoes. The contents of the paintings of those periods almost always reflected the interests or the occupation of those living in the house. In fact, some of the frescoes were found superimposed showing, that as they changed owners, the houses were re-decorated according to the interests of the new owner.

The first fresco is of Dionysus. Since drama evolved from Dionysiac festivals, the owner of that house could have been involved in drama or maybe another form of art. The fresco in the center is a representation of a white marble column in front of a marble-faced wall. It has no particular character. The owner could have been interested in impressive appearances and may have chosen this picture to show what he thought was great art.

The third fresco is of Demeter, the goddess of grain, being protected by snakes who are warding off evil. The snakes could be interpreted as the symbol of medicine, as well, so the owner of this house could have been a doctor or in some way involved with medicine.

The houses were big and adorned with colossal, heavy marble furniture, which was difficult to carry from one room to another. So, for practical reasons, they designed portable furniture. The stool can be folded not once but twice to take up almost no space. The table can also be folded into one small block. Still, with such simple furniture, the developed taste for graceful beauty can easily be seen in the refined decorations at the upper part of the table.

The bronze statuette of the Boy on a Dolphin is one of the best preserved artifacts of the museum. Water was used as a decorative element for both the public places and the houses. In the small fountains in the houses similar figures would stand in the center and the water which came through the eyes of the Dolphin and through the holes at the end of the feet of the boy would sprinkle in the most picturesque manner.

There is a story related to this particular combination of a boy and a dolphin. There was a woman living not too far from Ephesus. The people there were (and still are) making their living off sponge diving. This dangerous job takes the lives of many people in the depths of the sea. This one woman had lost nearly all of the male members of her family in the sea. But when the boy reached the age of 6 or 7 he wanted to prove that he was a big boy who did not need to listen·to the advice of his mother. He went to sea with his friends and never came back. The mother was very sad. She shut herself in a room and cried there for months. After a while, her friends decided to comfort her, they knocked on her door and told her that there was no need for her to cry any more because they had seen her boy riding on a dolphin, safe and sound. The mother was very happy. She opened the door to see him but her eyes were very weak from crying so she could not take the bright sun and she went blind. Her friends then made the statue with the boy on the dolphin so the mother could feel it and believe her son was truly safe and sound riding on the dolphin.

The statues of Hygeia and Ausculapius are standing side by side. Museums are, naturally, not the places to visit to appreciate only the art value or historic value of the things being displayed. They can be very educational from different aspects, too. One can have a better understanding of a concept or a word through these visits. If we can look at these statues from that point of view we can get a better understanding of one very important concept. Freudian psychology emphasizes two complexes: One is the Oedipus complex where the relation of a son and his mother is concerned, and the other is the Electra complex, where the close unbreakable relationship of a daughter with her father is emphasized. Aesculaius is the god of health and Hygeia, who stands for hygiene, is his daughter. Looking at these two statues, we can understand why hygiene is a must for health.

THE BRONZE STATUE OF AN EGYPTIAN PRIEST

We have said that everything in these houses was found to date to the Roman Period. This statue, however, dates to the Fifth Century B.C. This is not necessarily a contradiction, it just shows that whoever owned this statue must have been an antique dealer or, more probable, had a private collection of antiques in his house. The static figure of the priest is decorated with a panther skin hanging from his shoulder, hieroglyphics on various parts and a figure of a goddess on his right shoulder. Please keep in mind the posture of this goddess figure. A reference will be made to that later when discussing Artemis of Ephesus.

THE STATUE OF PRIAPOS

Phallic figures and statues of Priapos represent a dramatic love story of mythology. The wife of Zeus, Hera, was deeply in love with Adonis, famous for his great beauty. Hera was too frightened of Zeus to openly express this love but, day after day, every time she was looking for her husband, she would see smiles on the faces of the people... who were telling her that he might be with Leo with Leto,or with many others. Finally, Hera decided she, too, would not remain faithful, that she would go and find Adonis - with whom she had been in love with platonically for ages. She went to his house, knocked on the door, and said, "Guess who is here.", trying to sound very sweet and sexy. But the answer came not from Adonis but from another woman. At first,

Hera panicked, then she pulled herself together, thinking the sound behind the door could be that of one of the slaves. Her optimism did not last long once the door was opened. Hera saw that the one she hoped would be a slave was the most beautiful woman of the gods' family. She was Aphrodite. Not only was she there, but she was there with a baby in her arms. So she must have been in the house of the man Hera loved for a long time. Hera, jealous as she was, wanted to punish Aphrodite, tear her beauty apart. But the powers of these two goddesses were equal so Hera could do nothing to her. Hera, to get her revenge, cursed the baby in the arms of the beautiful Aphrodite and put him in this form, with an exaggerated penis. This poor little baby was given to a town so he could be raised by mortals and so he could learn the mentality of human beings.

An Egyptian Priest.
The goddess figure on the back
of his right shoulder has the similar
posture to Artemis of Ephesus.

Priapos, God of fertility.

In Lapseki, a town not too far from Troy, in the northwest of Turkey, the townspeople were not happy with this boy because, even at the age of four, he was flirting with the women and girls of the town. The men held a meeting, trying to decide how to kill this little monster. One would say his flesh needed to be pinched out, one would say his head needed to be chopped off, but the oldest member of the assembly had a better idea. He said they should let nature take care of him. He was only four years old, surely he was not going to be able to cope with nature. They all liked this idea. After all, nobody in the village wanted to get his hands bloody. They took the little boy into the forest.

Content and happy, the villagers returned to their village only to find out they were all cursed. All the men had become like the little boy. Only then did they realize that the person they had been trying to punish was really a god. Then all the villagers rushed to the forest - hoping to find him before nature took care of him. Once they found Priapos they decorated him with fruits, vegetables, and everything else that stood for fertility. He was worshipped as a god after that. The marble statue in the glass case depicts him with symbols of fertility.

The glass case next to the famous comedy writer, Menander, has few items on display. The terra-cotta toys, dice and various weights to be put underneath a spindle to get a finer thread are not too different from what people are using today for the same purposes.

PAN FLUTE

The bone flute in the lower corner looks similar to a regular flute but it is not quite the same as a shepherd would use today. The story related to such flutes is a sad one. Pan was a shepherd. He used to go out into the wilderness to graze his animals. Not to get bored, Pan used to play a flute. After a while,

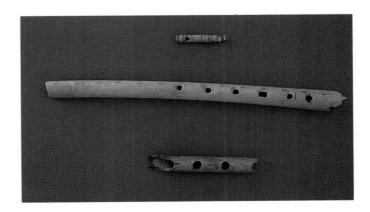

"Pan flute"

his flute sounded very monotonous to him so Pan tried to get better music. Of bones, wood, or straw he carved out a flute with one mouthpiece and two sides. When he played his flute now the beautiful tones spread out in the air. It did not take long for the rumours of the music to reach Apollo. The word was going around that the music of Pan's flute was better than that of Apollo's golden lyre. Apollo could not take the competition. He declared, "We need to have a contest. A Jury should decide on this matter. Once the jury decides whom is better then I want no more rumors on the subject."

The contest was held. Poor Pan, not knowing what was going on, was asked to play his flute. At first, he was a bit nervous but later he started playing the flute as nicely as ever. It sounded so nice that Apollo immediately knew that the decision of the jury would not be in his favor. Apollo became very angry and wanted to kill Pan. Pan was terribly frightened (We call this type of fear Panic. If one gets Panicked then he will be caught by whatever he is running away from... as did Pan.) and was caught by Apollo. Apollo not only killed Pan but blew him into a big drum which hung in front of a cave. Every time the wind would blow over Pan he would make such a terrible drum drum drum

119

sound that nobody would ever remember the nice sound of his flute. At least, that is what Apollo thought. But Apollo was wrong because, though hanging in front of the cave Pan did not make nice sounds, the nymphs remembered how nice it used to be to listen to Pan and they cried. From their teardrops the Meander River was formed.

SOCRATES

There is a fresco and a head of Socrates. They both date to the Fourth-Fifth Century A.D.

THE STATUE OF ARTEMIS

This Artemis is represented as a young woman. The features of this goddess, in all aspects, are identical to those of a human being. This is a typical

Artemis of Ephesus
Anatolian.

Artemis of the huntress
Greek.

characteristic of the Greek-originated god or goddess figure. At this spot it might be a good idea to compare the form of the figure and the values for which that form stands. In the two Artemis (Diana) statues, the Artemis of Ephesus and Artemis, the huntress, the differences and the similarities will be the differences and the similarities of the cultures which created them... namely, Anatolian civilizations and Greek civilizations.

THE KITCHEN UTENSILS

In the pit in the floor there are various items which were used in the kitchens.

A grinder to break wheat, to cook something similar to what we still eat in Anatolia, bulgur.

The terra-cotta pot with holes, an early sieve to wash the wheat.

Amphora, used to store wine and oil.

THE HALL OF THE FOUNTAIN RELICS

Every statue displayed in this hall used to be part of the fountains which decorated and cooled Ephesus through the centuries between the First Century B.C. to the Sixth Century A.D.

The Resting Warrior was used as a base for the column that rested on his head. The flat part on top of his head gives more or less the size of the column. The figure is resting on his left arm as though he was getting the strength from that arm to carry the column.

THE POLYPHEMUS GROUP STATUE

This group of statues was originally located in the Temple of Augustus at

The resting worrior.

the State Agora but later it was replaced in the Fountain of Pollio The fountain had a semi-circular wall as a backdrop for the set of statues. They were placed on a platform right over the pool of the fountain, allowing the reflection of the statues in the water.

The story told here is a Homeric story about Odysseus (Ulysses). Ulysses ended up in the cave of the giant Cyclops on the islands of Sicily. The Cyclops, Polyphemus, had killed many of Ulysses' friends and Ulysses wanted revenge. He knew he wouldn't be able to do it by force so he decided to trick the giant. One of his friends scooped out all the wine they had with them. (The first statue) The other one delivered the wine. (The second statue) Ulysses offered the wine to the giant until Polyphemus was drunk. Once the giant was drunk then the other friends of Ulysses poked a big branch of an olive tree into the single eye of the Cyclops. The Cyclops fell to the earth, shouting, "Who has done this?" He was shouting with such a big voice that Ulysses was frightened and all he could say was, "Nobody." The giant, who was not as great in wisdom as he was in size, continued shouting, "Nobody has harmed me, Nobody has harmed me." The friends of the giant, who could not see him but could hear him, answered him, "If nobody has harmed you, why in the world are you shouting like mad?" and none of his friends came to rescue Polyphemus.

In the meantime, sneaking underneath the goats, Ulysses and his friends escaped from the cave and went back to their boat where they felt courageous again. Ulysses shouted at the giant, "It was not Nobody who hurt you, it was me, Ulysses. I have my revenge for my dead friends." Finally the giant realized what had happened and wanted to sink the boat. From a hilltop, he rolled a big rock toward the boat. But, since he could not see, the rock missed the boat and Ulysses and his friends went on for another adventure in their Odyssey.

The statues which once
decorated the Fountain of Trajan.

The statues from the Fountain of Trajan decorated the first and second stories of this fountain. There, two of the Venus statues were standing at either side of the protruded section of the 'U' -shaped construction. The legendary founder of Ephesus, Androklos, Dionysus, members of the royal family, and satyrs contributed to the impressive appearance of the building.

The other set of statues are the Nymphs. Since water was running over these statues where they were used as a decorative element, the dresses of these three Nymphs appear to be sticking to the bodies of the statues.

The last set of statues belong to three other women who were part of the Water Palace in Ephesus.

ROOM NUMBER THREE

To the left of the entrance of the hall, small objects dated to the Byzantine Period are displayed. The white glazed bowl is decorated with a bird which was associated with Christ. The bird with a red spot on her chest was supposedly feeding her starving babies with her own flesh and blood from her chest. The fragment of an icon represents the bishops. The Iconoclastic Period had ended by the Tenth Century A.D. so this fragment of an icon can be dated not any earlier than the Tenth Century.

There is a rich coin collection in the next room. On the coins which were printed in Ephesus there are two common designs. On the wall, the enlarged copies of an Ephesian coin shows those. One side of the coin shows a bee and on the other side there is the figure of the Mother Goddess Artemis. The name of the city, Ephesus, was derived from a Hittite word, Apasas, meaning 'bee". Thus, the bee is the symbol for the name of the city, Ephesus. The Mother Goddess Artemis Ephesia is the Ephesian interpretation of the ancient Anatolian goddess, Cybele. But, over the centuries, Artemis Ephesia acquired such a unique personality that her name, though respected by many others, was associated with the city of Ephesus more than of any other of her followers. She became the symbol of the town. So, on the coins, we have on the one side the image of Artemis, the symbol of the town, and on the other side there is

The Nymphs.

the bee, the symbol for the name of the town.

THE GLASS TRAY

In some of the places in Ephesus, when the color of the stained glass could be added to the picture of the site, one might get a very vivid image... as when the dim light projecting over the stage of the Odeon is seen, or a red, romantic color used lighting the comfortable sofa in the brothel needs to be imagined with the right hue.

This blue, glass tray is helping one appreciate their talent in using natural dyes to color glass. Apart from its attraction due to the perfect coloring, the design, once more, sets an example for the refined taste of creating beauty in simplicity.

Drinking wine was an indispensable part of the lifestyle when Ephesus was living its Glamorous Periods. The collection of wine cups shows the number of different designs they have created to consume this drink. The residue in one of the cups is the genuine wine residue of the drink found in a two-thousand year old wine barrel, or amphora.

The snake was found in front of a house. The head part is missing. It was probably used to scare off evil from the house. It was gold-plated, there are still a few remains of gold which can be seen if examined closely.

To the left of the entrance, on the wall, the masks are displayed. Though the upper part of the faces look similar in all five marble masks, the formation of the mouth is different in each one and, with that difference, they were able to create varying expressions like anger, fear, astonishment, sadness, and surprise (or shock).

Priapos, he was decorated fruits and flowers to symbolize fertility.

The God of Health.

The collection of oil lamps is quite rich. Oil lamps were mass produced by the use of molds. They were one of the main trade items for the Ephesians. They were sometimes able to get creative with the decoration of the lamp but only on the surface. The actual technique of getting light remained the same for ages. The collection shows the oil lamps from the Sixth Century B.C. up until the Sixth Century A.D. This is 12 hundred years and, as one can easily see, there were no major changes in the method of getting light.

The Ivory Frieze is a masterpiece of two things. First of all, it is a masterpiece of an ivory work. Provided they had no electrical tools to work on such a hard

material, the fine detail achieved must have required undeniable artistic talent. They were able to get a three-dimensional look in the relief by the combination of high and low reliefs perfectly blending in with each other. The expressions on the faces are so real that one has no doubt in identifying what the figures stand for. On the glass panel on the left, the figure in the middle is that of a dying man. He is not dead yet because his muscles are still tense, holding onto the sword. But, looking at the expression on his face, you can be sure that he is giving his last breath.

The frieze is a masterpiece for another reason, patience. When this furniture decoration was found it was in thousands of pieces. What was left of it could fill the palms of your two hands. But the restorers, with no pattern to follow, with lots of creativity, a bit of luck, and with an enormous amount of patience, put this masterpiece back together.

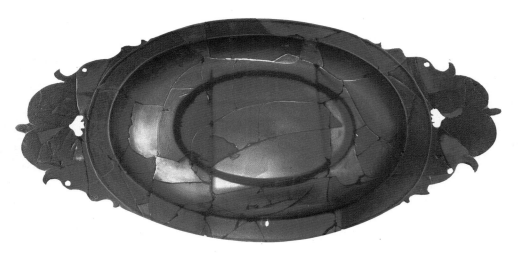

The glass tray.
The color of the glass reflects the ability of the
Ephesians in staining the glass.

The story which is being told on the frieze is about a battle fought during the reign of Emperor Trajan (98-117 A.D.)

THE COURTYARD

Next to the door before the book stand the marble block has an illustration of a hand stretching on the corner, a man trying to sacrifice a boy. The scene is taken from the story of Abraham, who was trying to keep his promise to God by sacrificing his only son Isaac. God holds his hand out, saying, "Stop. Sacrifice the sheep, instead."

The sundial, in the center of the courtyard, was dedicated to the mother of Emperor Caracalla, Julia Domna. Caracalla (188-217 A.D.) had asked the Oracles to prophesize about his future. The prophecy was an unpleasant one, he was told his brother, Geta, would take his place. At first, Caracalla did not pay much attention to what the Oracles had told him but, when Geta started acquiring quite a bit of power and respect, Caracalla killed his brother. The mother was terribly upset and she began to do very wicked things. Feeling guilty, Caracalla consulted the Oracles again, hoping to find a cure for his mother. The cure was to give valuable gifts to Julia Domna. This sundial could have been one of those gifts dedicated to this unlucky mother.

The sarcophagus next to the sundial must have belonged to someone who was involved in the fine arts because the decorations of the tomb depict the goddesses of the fine arts, the Musea (the Muses). Of the nine Musea, only the Musea of music, literature, and drama were illustrated. The large sarcophagus, with a statue of the owner reclining on it, was found where the marble quarry of the town was. The Third Century fashion for sarcophagus was to add the statue of the dead or the family of the dead onto the top.

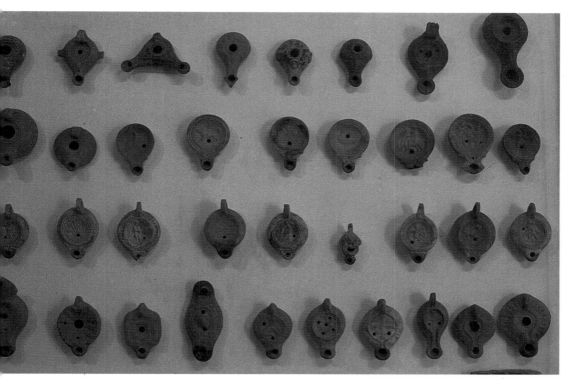

The oil Lamps.

The big marble block facing the book stand has an inscription about the customs regulations which were announced on July 9, 62 during the reign of Emperor Nero.

"The rights of the revenue collectors in the Asian Customs. The customs and other revenues will be collected not by civil servants but by agencies who have paid cash in advance to do the job. The Customs is equal to 2.5% of the goods. Luxury tax is 5%..."

THE HALL OF THE FUNERARY RELICS
One way of identifying the different cultures, religions, and civilizations is through the differences of their burial ceremonies and the types of tombs. Some liked to be buried with food and water so they could feed themselves

in the other world; some liked to have their valuables, even their wives, buried with the dead body; some wanted to be laid simply on the ground; and yet others chose to be cremated. Each type of burial, of course, developed a different shape and material for interment. For some people, the terracotta or sliver urns were enough to hold their ashes. For some others, monumental tombs were not sufficient to express how 'great' a person he or she was.

The chart, on the wall to the left of the door, gives only a few of the many, many different kinds of burial arrangements in Anatolia... sort of underlining the fact that there were so many different civilizations in Anatolia.

One of these illustrations is quite unique because it is the illustration of one of the seven wonders of the world, the Mausoleum. Mausolus was the king of Halicarnassus (Bodrum). When he died, in 353 B.C., his wife, Artemisia II, wanted to show her love for her husband by building a great memorial tomb. She called this tomb the Mausoleum, meaning the house of Mausolus. (the '-eum' ending means the house of... as in Museum, the house of the Musea...

The Ivory Frieze.
The expression on the faces of the figures
are as real as alive.

Artemisium, the house of Artem's... etc.) Later, however, the word mausoleum was used to describe a tomb with the architectural characteristics of the original Mausoleum - which are a high, square podium, with columns supporting a pyramidal roof, and a statue of a horse or a chariot with more than one horse at the very top.

A tomb could be magnificent and monumental but not necessarily a mausoleum. The difference between a Monumental tomb and a mausoleum can be seen on the illustrations on this chart.

In the window across from the chart, there is a display of Mycenean bowls and cups which date to the Thirteenth and Fourteenth Centuries B.C. To have such items in Ephesus shows that, as early as 33, 34 hundred years before our time, people were living here and were not simple settlers in the area but developed enough to carry on overseas trade with the Myceneans.

It is not just what they were buried in but what they were buried with that has always interested the historians. The historians were able to get an idea about the people they were trying to study, a people from the depths of history. One tradition they found was quite interesting and was very expressive of personal feelings.

When the husband was dead, the wife was expected to cry in a 'tear drop' bottle to show her loyalty. There was, however, no regulation as to the size of such 'tear drop' containers. The tiny bottle on the left hand side of the window of such bottles will tell you how loyal some wives could be...

In the corner, next to the steps, the evolution of the mother goddess in Anatolia is described.

From the Palaeolithic Era on, food and childbirth were the essential needs for survival. When the effect (the birth) was removed from the cause (impregnation and conception) by a lapse of nine months, it was quite impossible to discover a connection between these two functions. As women were seen bearing children continually, they were believed to be the essential

life producers. It was woman who conserved and promoted the abundance and continuance of the species. Therefore, the Great Mother Goddess cult was spread all over the inhabited areas and developed only slight, regional variations. In Anatolia, one thing remained common to different representations of the Mother Goddess, an image of a lion as a representative of power accompanied her in most descriptions.

The statue in the niche belongs to the Mother Goddess of Anatolia... Cybele, goddess of female fruitfulness and recipient of furiously orgiastic and ecstatic worship. Female fruitfulness was not necessarily just bearing children but, just as important, giving affection, love, an endless ability to protect, self-sacrifice, and consideration were also attributes of a Mother deity.

In Anatolia, where the worship of the Mother Goddess was very extensive, matriarchy is an everlasting tradition. This Anatolian tradition developed a vocabulary which is still being used to identify the difference between a mother as a female parent and a mother, or a woman, with qualities ranging beyond being just the bearer of a child. The first one is called 'ANNE' and the second one is called 'ANA', as in:

ANA Tanrica   - Mother Goddess.

Meryem ANA   The Virgin Mary, the Holy Mother.

ANADOLU   Anatolia - the cultural and historical name used to describe Asia Minor, Turkey... it means 'full of mothers'.

THE HALL OF ARTEMIS

When the Ephesians completed the Temple of Artemis in the Seventh Century B.C., they introduced this temple to the known world as the biggest

The Hand of the God
Abraham and his son, Isaac.

house ever built in the name of any one mother goddess. They said, "It does not matter by which name you call your mother goddess, it could be Isis in Egypt, Astarte in Mesopotamia, Cybele in Anatolia, or Rhea in Greece. Your Mother Goddess is living here." So, Artemis possessed not only most of the attributes of an Anatolian Mother Goddess, Cybele, but she also incorporated most of the features of the deities of Egypt, Mesopotamia, Persia, and Minoa.

The display in the glass case shows the variety of origins of the offerings which came to the temple. They are typical works of art from Egypt to Greece around the Fertile Crescent (the land around the eastern end of the

Mediterranean.) Her idol is a good representation of the synthesis of many different concepts and deities. She wore three super imposed crowns of castles or city walls. She was a civic deity, the protectress of cities. In addition to many Anatolian cities, she was the protectress of Marseilles and Syracusa. She was the goddess of severe beauty and prominent stature. Her faraway look, disdaining the horizon, seemed to be lost in eternity. Behind her head there is the disc of a full moon. The Phoenician goddess, Astarte (Ashtoreth) was the goddess of fertility and the stars. In fact, the word 'star' could have been derived from her name.

The Mother, "Ana",
The one who gives everything:
Fertility, Prosperity, Love.
The Anatolian goddess, Cybele.

Since they did not know the difference between the moon and the stars, it was thought the goddess of the stars should be represented by the brightest 'star', the moon. Since Astarte was identified with Artemis, Artemis is wearing the symbol of Astarte, the moon.

On her upper chest, there are human figures, illustrating the features of the different deities of various geographic locations. But, she is also representing the sacred concepts prior to the personification of the deities, she could be a pillar of deep-rooted traditions of many lands, too. Before gods were regarded in human form, objects which were thought to be related to supernatural powers were worshipped. The tradition which related to Artemis is the worship of a meteor as a diopete, or sacred stone. People could not identify what the stone was so they thought it must have been the 'reflection from heaven' and they worshipped it.

The replacement of that worship is defined in the signs of the Zodiac she

Artemis of Ephesus.

is wearing as a necklace. One of her titles, mentioned in Chapter nineteen of the Acts of St. Paul is 'Diana and the image which fell down from Jupiter.' On her arms, the inevitable lions can be seen... as any other Anatolian mother goddess would wear. The breast-like figures may represent a crowd of male bees impregnating her, as she was considered a Queen Bee. Another interpretation is that they are the testicles of the bulls sacrificed in ceremonies conducted by the priests. They could symbolize the number of bulls sacrificed to show how much she was being respected or, according to one belief, the Goddess was being fertilized through the offering of semen. Some theories

are that the breasts are merely that, showing her great capacity for motherhood.

Although fertilized by the power of life, as perhaps symbolized by the bulls' seed, she remained ever a virgin. These breasts, bees, or testicles in her various idols were never less than eleven and not more than forty-four.

From the waist down to her feet, she is wearing a skirt which is divided by parallel, perpendicular and horizontal lines. The creatures, real and mythological, are represented as though verifying her virtue as the protectress of all creatures, the mother of all.

When the values for which the Temple of Artemis were changed the temple became nothing more than a good source of marble. The grandeur of the construction was no longer interesting to people as a wonder of the world and the pieces of marble were torn from the temple as though setting a sad example of the cruelty of intolerance for different beliefs. The example of this destruction can be seen on the block of stone placed on the corner of the hall by the steps going up to the next room. The side of the block facing the

The cross on the marble
block of the Temple of Artemis.

big Artemis statue is decorated with the typical hellenistic ornaments, the eggs and darts. The rest of the surface was shaved off. The end of the block facing the steps has an illustration of a cross. This marble block, which was originally quarried out in the Fourth Century B.C. for the construction of the Temple of Artemis, was used some nine hundred years later for the construction of a church.

THE HALL OF THE IMPERIAL CULTS AND PORTRAITS

The first of the three portraits displayed on the wall next to the Hall of Artemis is of a half-breed negro. The native race in Anatolia is predominantly white so this person's parents must have come or been brought from another place. But, to have a statue of a half-breed can suggest that inter-racial marriage was accepted and the offspring of such marriages were respected to an extent that statues could be made of them.

On the frieze from the Temple of Hadrian the reliefs depict the legends of the foundation of the city... Androklos, chasing the boar who was frightened of the fire which was started by a fish, the Amazons, the first ones to settle in the area, and Dionysiac processions, various deities, and royal figures.

The statues of Augustus and his wife, Livia, at the far end of the hall, are sitting there as though they are trying to give the message that not everybody was as bad as those who destroyed the Temple of Artemis and disregarded the artistic value of the edifice. Augustus and Livia had given the Christians a very difficult time but, even after the Christians grew strong enough some four hundred years after these two had died and they could have easily destroyed the statues for revenge, the statues were preserved. Some people respected the art value of these statues and found a simple but efficient manner of protecting them. A cross was put on the forehead of each statue, the statues were Christianized, and thus were saved from an attempt of destruction. This creativity can show there is no limit to what one can do if he thinks constructively.

The women warriors, the Amazons.

A Half breed Negro.

135

ARTEMISIUM
(THE TEMPLE
OF ARTEMIS)

In the second millennium, apart from images similar to human form, objects of doubtful origin would be explained away as having fallen from heaven and were paid divine honor. The sacred stone, the diopete, was kept in the trunk of a tree which was also accepted as a sacred object. The Amazons, the women warriors who were the first to settle in Ephesus, came to worship the diopete in the sacred tree (in the grove where the Temple of Artemis was to be built many hundreds of years later). The Amazons had taken the protection of the holy grove under their own responsibility. In the hymn to Artemis by Callimachus, it was said,

"For thee, too, the Amazons whose mind is set on war, In Ephesus beside the sea established an image beneath an oak trunk, and Hippo performed a holy rite for thee, and they themselves around the image danced in shields and armor."

(Cevat Şakir, ASIA MINOR)

During the middle of the first millennium most holy objects were personified. The xoanon, the sacred tree, was anthropomorphosized and the grove of the holy diopete became the sanctuary for the cult of Artemis. The earliest statues of Artemis were all carved from a tree as a continuation of the old tradition. The priestesses, named Kosmiteirai, were responsible for decorating the wooden statue with robes and ornaments for sacred processions. This is the reason the Roman copies of the goddess are not identical, though the basic character is the same.

It is supposed that the Amazons founded the first shrine. The first marble temple was not built until the mid of the Seventh Century. The temple, which was considered to be one of the seven wonders of the world, was built in the middle of the Sixth Century. The architects, Chersiphron and Mategenes, were confronted with two big challenges. First, they had to overcome a natural difficulty. The area, which was once a grove, had become nothing more than a marshland by the sea. To get a solid, sturdy foundation they used coal and animal hide. The second challenge was to build the temple bigger than any other temple that had ever been built before. By using 127 columns, which measured 15 meters in height, they were able to achieve the majestic size. Having so many columns was like recreating the trees of the grove from stone. The temple was completed after more than two centuries. Painters, sculptors, and all the other craftsmen of Anatolia competed with each other to contribute something more beautiful - each of which won unanimous admiration.

The temple was able to give many people an eternal name. One of those who wanted his name linked through history with the temple was an idiot named Herostratos. He set the temple on fire on the 21st of may, the the night when Alexander the Great was born.

The restoration of the temple was not easy. They could use the financial support in terms of contributions but when Alexander the Great offered his contribution he stated one condition. His name was to be inscribed on the facade on the new temple. No... the temple was to be built in the name of the Mother

The Temple of Artemis.
The Church of St. John. The Mosque of İsabey.

Goddess... Alexander was cleverly refused and the Ephesians were able to restore the Temple. The destructions of nature or of an idiot were reparable because the people who respected and believed in an idea worked hard to create...and they created wonders.

However, when the destruction comes from intolerance of ideas and the changing of values the destruction is without repair. Unfortunately, the Temple of Artemis, the construction which was once an inspiration for creation, was leveled to the earth and completely destroyed by the christians. Their justification was very simple. The temple did not stand for the values of their religion. Starting from the Fifth Century, the sanctuary, once the holy grove, began to be buried in the mud. But Artemis, once an oak tree, was too valuable for the local traditions to be lost in history just because a few decided not to respect her house. In the Artemisium she kept her identity, she was still the Mother. She was still the Virgin. She was still the lady of Ephesus. And, since 431, when the Ecumenical Council met in Ephesus, she became the Virgin Mary.

THE VIRGIN MARY'S HOUSE

There are no archeological evidences to prove the Virgin Mary ever spent her last years here. Neither a sarcophagus with her name nor an inscription dated to the time of her reputed presence in Ephesus were found around the city. However, in some cases religious legends, traditions, and literature from the early ages of the Church can be used to determine whether or not a place is a Biblical site.

Mary's presence in a place close to John's activity would seem to have been assured because of Christ's commission given to St. John from the cross, "Behold thy Mother!" and the passage continued, written by John long after Mary's assumption, to confirm the result by saying, "And from that hour that disciple took her unto his own home." St. John spent the last years of his life in Ephesus. If John's area of apostalic work centered about Ephesus then, being under his care, Mary would have lived there, too.

Mary Magdalen's life had been, coincidentally or otherwise, involved with the concept of resurrection. St.Mary Magdalen was an eyewitness of the first evidence of the resurrection offered by God, according to Christian belief, in the person of her brother, Lazarus. It was, again, she who discovered the empty tomb of Jesus and brought the news to Peter and John. It seems as though Providence reserved for Mary Magdalen a special place in the mystery of resurrection. In the Bible, addressing Magdalen, it says "...go to my brethren, and say to them..." The informing of others of the resurrection was given to her as a mission. She had been directly and personally implicated in the main manifestation of resurrection. We may, then, say... where there is a sign of resurrection, there had to be Magdalen, or the other way around... where there was Magdalen, there must be some evidence of the resurrection.

The combination of the Virgin Mary, St. John, and St. Mary Magdalen has been referred to as 'the second holy family', formed at the foot of the cross. St. Gregory of Tours (538-594) wrote, "In Ephesus is found the place where the apostle John wrote the Gospel... in that city Mary Magdalen rests." The presence of Magdalen's tomb in Ephesus suggests at least a conjecture that she, too, traveled with Mary and John. The Patriarch of Jerusalem, Modestus (630-634), wrote that Mary Magdalen went to John after the death of the Virgin to inform him of her death. As a proven historic fact, there is no basis. But, if St. John was in Ephesus, with a tomb in the Grotto of the Seven Sleepers,and if Mary Magdalen was in Ephesus, then it is most likely that the Virgin Mary died in Ephesus.

In the middle of the Fourth Century, a building in Ephesus was converted into a church. This great Basilica was the Cathedral of Ephesus, the Church

The Virgin Mary's House.

of the Virgin Mary. The identification is assured by a long inscription of Bishop Hypatius' found in the natex. In the early times of Christianity a church was named after a person only if he or she lived in that locality. Having the Church of the Virgin Mary in Ephesus confirms her presence here through a religious tradition.

The Ecumenical Council of 431 A.D. was held in the Church of the Virgin Mary in Ephesus. Although other Councils were usually held in Nycia, for this particular Council they picked Ephesus. The dogma decided upon in Ephesus was the Divine Motherhood of the Virgin Mary. If there were no tradition of

Mary's being in Ephesus then why should they have chosen Ephesus to decide on this particular subject?

Local traditions are handed down from generation to generation. One of those traditions faithfully transmitted from the elder to the young is to make an annual pilgrimage to the House of the Virgin Mary on August 15th to commemorate the Assumption of the Virgin Mary. If Ephesus were without a tradition of this belief then from what motives and by whom and why should this curious tradition be invented?

Another question solved by the tradition is that of the comparative superior state of preservation of Mary's home. The peasants can be credited not only

The Church of the Virgin Mary. In the early times of Christianity a church would be named after a person only if he or she had lived in that locality.

with the preservation of the tradition but also with the preservation of the house itself.

The place where the Virgin Mary lived for the last nine years of her life, the place of her Dormition, the site of her Assumption, was discovered through Anne Catherine Emmerich. Sister Emmerich had never left Germany but she had visions of the house. The Lazarists, in their scientific expeditions, used her revelations to locate Mary's house. Catherine pictured the house and described it in 1821 but it was not discovered until 1891. In 1967, Pope Paul VI, and in 1979, Pope John Paul, II, visited the house and both confirmed the importance of the house for the Christian world. The house of the Virgin, however, is important not only for the Christians. The native Moslems respect the site very much and visit the house, hoping the Virgin Mary will help them with their problems. It is a very common sight to see a Christian kneeling in front of the apse while a Moslem, next to his shoulder, is carrying on his ritual of prayer.

The water which comes from the spring under the house is believed to have therapeutic power. People from all over the world visit the house and drink the water, hoping for the recovery of their illness. The glass case in the house, displaying the badges, rings, and bracelets of many sorts, is an example of how people of many different nationalities show their gratitude to Mary by offering their valuables.

The Divine Motherhood of Mary
was accepted in this church Ephesus in 431 AD.

Looking at the stone building from outside, one can see a red line running along the wall of the house. The wall below this red line is made up of stonework dating to the First Century A.D. so those stones must have belonged to the original house. During the Sixth Century, the Byzantines restored many buildings of religious importance. The upper part of the red line dates to this period. Obviously, the building was an important edifice then, too, to deserve this restoration.

The narrow entrance of the building, which is now being used as a chapel, leads to the room wich was once the Living room of the house.

The two square, grey marble stones on the pavement right under the arch in front of the apse cover an area where ashes were found. It must have been the place where the hearth of the house was. The original house was in 'cross' shape. Now there is a room only on one side of the cross. That room, according to the visions of Catherine Emmerich, was the bedroom. The spring comes from beneath the pink stones in this room.

In the small niche to the left of the altar with the statue of the Virgin Mary there is a bronze figure which was given to the chapel by Pope Paul VI, on his visit to the house.

The whole area around the house is so peaceful and has such a very tranquil atmosphere that it is like an open-air sanctuary. One will notice the ribbons and colorful material tied to the branches of the trees, which are like the pillars of this sanctuary. These colorful things tied on the trees are the of-

The Church of the Virgin Mary.

ferings left there by those whose wishes have come true. Giving offerings to the gods for something that has been asked of them is as old a tradition as the history of religion. The names of the religions and gods, the number of gods in the different religions can change over the centuries but the traditions remain more or less the same. In this region, when it was the Mother Goddess Cybele helping the people, the offerings were animal sacrifices, to protect and give out prosperity, the Mother Goddess Artemis of Ephesus was content with gold and valuable gifts, and Mother Mary, whose divine motherhood was accepted here, keeps being generous in making people happy and healthy with nothing more than these small offerings.

THE CITY WALLS AND THE PERSECUTION GATE

During the Eleventh Century, the harbour of Ephesus was silted in. The marshland was a terrible source of malaria and the inhabitants of Ephesus were forced to leave the city. They could have picked one of the other hills in the valley to settle on but, because of the religious importance of this hill, Ayasoluk (where the tomb of St. John was located), they moved here. The ancient buildings were a sufficient source of material for the construction of the fortification. One of the three gates of the wall still gives an access to the settlement of the fourth city of Ephesus.

The decorative pieces, too, were taken from the antique sources, mainly from sarcophagi. One frieze decorating the wall over the entrance arch was depicting a scene from the Trojan Wars, where Hector was being dragged by Achilles. Since Christian persecution had always been a dramatic issue for the historians and the archeologists, the scene — without further investigation — was associated with that persecution when the gate was first excavated in the last century. Now it is known, though, that the gate was not the place where one belief was being kept alive in spite of the death of another but it is still called the Persecution Gate.

''persecution!!''

144

THE BASILICA OF ST. JOHN

After the Crucifixion, the disciples of Jesus Christ left Jerusalem. Saint John was banished to Patmos, an island not too far from the Aegean coast of Anatolia. While St. John was in his cave, he heard a sound. When he turned around to see who had spoken to him, he saw a man with a cloak which reached down to his feet, which were like burnished brass. His white beard came down to his chest and in his right hand he held seven stars and behind him were seven golden candlesticks. He called himself Alpha and Omega, the beginning and the end. He was God. The seven stars were the angels of the seven churches; and the seven candlesticks are the seven churches. Saint John was given the task of writing down Christ's message for the seven churches of Asia (Ephesus, Smyrna, Pergamom, Tyatira, Sardis, Philadelphia, and Laodicea). [see Revelation, chapter one]

Following the assassination of Saint Paul, passing of the revelation to the seven churches was not sufficient, Saint John had to continue his sacred mission. He assumed the main responsibility for all the churches under the Church of Ephesus. He wrote much of his Gospel here. The traditions which were associated with St. John and Ephesus were of great importance in late Antiquity and during the Middle Ages. His burial place was revered from earliest times and became the site of a magnificent church.

In the middle of the Fourth Century, the construction of a small, square martyrion over the tomb of St. John was the first act of the triumphant church of Christian Ephesus. The tomb also gave rise to a legend, John was not dead but slept. It was believed he showed signs of life by scattering dust with his breath. The dust, called manna, was used to cure the sick. Every year, on May 8, the inhabitants of the area came in procession to lay flowers on the tomb of the Apostle. They apparently were transferring a pagan floral procession, the rhodismos, to the holy tomb. The day was an occasion for a great celebration and a nightlong mass. Considering the importance of the location for the pilgrims, Justinian and his wife, Theodora, (Byzantine emperor and empress) had the small church torn down and replaced it with a new and far more magnificent building. In terms of construction, the interior of the church of St. John was both massive and simple. It was in the form of a basilica.

There are two definitions of 'basilica'. One is that it is a church accorded certain liturgical privileges. The other definition is that it is a rectangular building divided into a nave and aisles and used as a hall of justice and for other political activities. To talk about their social and political problems the

Architecture similar to the
character of the Roman Basilicas

people used to meet in the basilica. The congregation was allocated to the end of the rectangular building where they would talk about their problems and they would reach decisions. In order for these decisions to be put into practice, they had to get the confirmation of the pontiff, the representative of the Roman Emperor. Since the Roman emperors had all been deified, the pontiffs were actually representatives of 'God'.

The pontiff was placed across from the congregation on the other end of the building. The spokesman of the pontiff carried on the liaison between the two ends, carrying on his duty on a slightly elevated platform called a tribune, located in the chancel or bema. The tribune extended from the pontiff's end of the basilica toward the congregation. There was an altar in front of the seat of the pontiff, (or pontifax). To conclude the ceremonies, marking the approval or disapproval of the Roman Emperor, through his pontiff, of the decisions made, sacrifices were made on the altar.

The Basilica type of construction was adopted in the early stages of Christianity for religious worship. The congregation of the church occupied the same section of the building as they had in the hall of justice. The representative of God, the cross, replaced the pontiff in the apse at the other end of the basilica (the Pope was granted the status of Pontifax Maximus, or Head Pontiff). The bishop of the church became the liaison and used the tribune, now the pulpit, to reach and communicate with the congregation. The altar was no longer used for sacrifice but candles were lift upon it as a symbolic offering to God.

The Church of St. John was built with the principle of the basilica in mind. It was an elaborate, cruciformed basilica with four domes over the central body of the building and two domes on each side where the building extended to give it the cross-shape. The remains of the tribune can be seen on the ground, extending halfway into the central nave. The steps in the center lead up to the grave area of St. John. The tomb of the evangelist can be reached by a

flight of steps from the place where the altar was in front of the apse.

The side aisles supported galleries and the narthex gave access to a large atrium, the courtyard. In the central nave, on the capitals of the restored set of columns, the names of the 'patrons' can be seen in the monograms of the Imperial couple, Justinian and Theodora.

The name of the architect of the church is inscribed on the marble block leaning on the brick wall next to the entrance of the narthex. Isidoro was a geometrician from Miletus. He also built the Church of Saint Sophia in Istanbul. The condition of these two churches can not even be compared. The Church of St. John is in ruins whereas the Church of St. Sophia is standing up proudly — as if denying the fifteen centuries which could have reduced it down to a small hill of rubble. In spite of similar natural disasters which the church of the apostle faced and could not resist, the Church of St. Sophia is still an intact wonder of architecture. It was the will of Man to keep it intact and 'alive' through the centuries. It was the Byzantines who created it, it was Ottomans who preserved it as a mosque, and it was Atatürk who changed it into a museum so art lovers of the whole world could be responsible for the future preservation of this beautiful building.

If the Church of St. John had been given similar attention then we would

Baptistry.

not now have to use our imaginations to figure out what it had looked like. Isidoro , the architect, makes us think, once again, what we could do if we wanted and wished to be constructive. We can keep our wonders or we can turn them into ruins...

The floor of the church was covered with mosaics of geometric design. Much of the interior was covered with frescoes. The marble work, paintings, and other decorative accents were wrought by artists from the capital of the Empire, Constantinople, now known as İstanbul. Although the church was completed in the time of Justinian (527-565), decoration was still being added later.

The baptistry is of octagonal plan. In the center there is a rather deep baptismal pool. The walls were faced with marble and the windows probably had plain white glass set in to comply with the act of baptism, purification. Those who were baptized were dressed in white robes, they walked into the pool from one end, submerged in the water, and came out as a new Christian.

Adjacent to the baptistry was a rectangular room with a mosaic floor. This was the place where the bishop presided as judge.

The addition of the room illustrates the elevation of the Church of St. John into the Cathedral Church of Ephesus.

THE MOSQUE OF İSA BEY

The mosque was built in 1375 and stands as a monument to and an early example of Turco-Islamic work. It is a massive, rectangular building with two domes and, before the earthquake in the Seventeenth Century, with two minarettes. The entrance has a very inviting beauty of stonework and the courtyard is decorated with columns which were ornated with the capitals taken from the antique temples. It makes one feel proud to see that, in this mosque, the stones of the temples were respected for their art value and not destroyed to be used as ordinary construction material just because they were created to beautify a building of a different form of worship.

Through a triple arch, there is the entrance into the enclosed portion of the mosque. The four domes rest on four columns. One of the columns is topped with an original capital brought from Ephesus, the others reflect the Turkish style, with stalactites.

The mosques are oriented toward Mecca, this can be seen in the orientation of the Mihrab, the niche in the middle of the wall opposite the entrance. The Mihrab, the domes, and the minarettes were all set-in with fine Turkish tiles, the remains can still be seen on the brickwork of the minarette.

PRIENNE

The earliest settlement in this city has been dated to the Twelfth Century B.C. The Cariens were the earliest ones to discover the advantages that the location of Prienne offered. Being by the Meander River and the Aegean Sea, Prienne supplied its settlers with a rich agricultural land, along with an unmatchable opportunity of sea transportation. Ionians migrated to the land (which would be called by their name from then on) in the Eleventh Century B.C. The city was founded by Aepytus or Philotas of Thebai. The historians, Strabon and Pausanias, did not agree upon who the founder was but they both mentioned that Prienne was one of the most important cities of the Ionian Confederation.

During the Seventh Century B.C., the Lydians ruled the city. The Lydian kings respected their value so, Prienne did not suffer from being ruled by another kingdom. However, in 546 B.C., when the Persians (after defeating the Lydians) took over the command in Ionia, Prienne, too, took an important role in the rebellion against the new rulers. The ultimate victory of the Persians was the beginning of the dark ages for Prienne.

After the Lade War (494 B.C.), the new city of Prienne was not possible to be founded until 350 B.C. The new town took Athens as an example. In the physical structure, as well as in the political structure, it is easy to trace the Athenian influence.

With Alexander the Great ruling over Anatolia, an autonomic society was not what the city-states could claim for their form of administration. Thus, Prienne was then but a small city of about 7000 people of the great Hellenistic Empire.

During Roman rule (starting from 190 B.C.), Prienne enjoyed the wealth and recognition of the Roman emperors, especially during the reign of Augustus.

Unfortunately, the sea kept receding and Prienne kept losing its importance. During the Byzantine Period (Fourth-Twelfth Centuries A.D.), Prienne was only a small bishopric with no more than 2000 people living in the city. After the Thirteenth Century, Prienne was completely abandoned.

The city was built on the Hippodomas plan, where all the streets either run parallel or cut each other in the perpendicular. The town was also known for the philosopher, Bias, who thought that the most valuable thing one could own was one's own ideas.

BOULEUTERION

In this rectangular building, which could seat about 640, all citizens who had the right to vote met at least once a year to elect the city magistrates.

THEATER

The orchestra is surrounded by a row of seats, reminding one of thrones, for the dignitaries of the town. In the middle there is an altar, dedicated to Dionysos. The auditorium can seat 5-6 thousand people.

TEMPLE OF ATHENA

The temple was built by Pytheos, who was the architect of one of the seven wonders of the world, the Mausoleum. The style is Ionic Peripteral, with six columns at the front and at the back and eleven on each side. It took more than a hundred years to finish this marvelous edifice and just one earthquake to destroy it.

MILETUS

The original site shows the remains of an early habitation by Mycenean settlers dating back to the Thirteenth or Fourteenth Century B.C. With the arrival of the Ionians, Milesians extended their authority over the hinterland, in spite of Carien resistance farther south. They were well-placed on their promontory, in sheltered waters and with very fertile valleys behind. The urge to have better markets and overseas trading centers brought about the colonization which extended their power from the harbors of the north of the Black Sea down to Egypt on the Nile River. The wealth they were able to acquire through their colonies helped them to remain independent of Lydia. It was this secure surrounding which enabled the development of philosophy and science in the work of Thales, Anaximander, Anaximenes, and Cadmus, the historian.

Like other Ionic cities, Miletus was involved in the Ionian revolt against the Persians in 494. The city suffered under the Persian invasion and could not make it up during the Period of Alexander the Great. They resisted Alexander and were severely punished by him. During the Roman Period (during the First Century B.C.), though no longer independent, Miletus became prosperous once more.

St. Paul's visit to Miletus came at tne end of his third journey to this area. When he spoke to the Ephesians, in addressing them as the 'elders of the church', he was trying to explain that Christianity was not a mystery religion, "I have kept back nothing; I have disclosed to you the whole purpose of God." (see Acts 20:27)

The end of the rich, prosperous city came about because its harbor silted in and its commerce stopped. During the Byzantine Period and under the rule of Selçuk until 1403, it constantly shrank in size and importance until it became the small town of Balat, which now has only a thousand inhabitants.

Miletus once had four harbors. These were not only very well-protected for the ships to be tied up but were arranged as commercial complexes with the commercial agoras built right next to them. The colonnaded stoas, fountains, and statues decorating the harbors gave the visitor an impression not only of wealth but of the city's abvious interest in the fine arts. Hippodomos of Miletus (who can be considered the father of city planning) must have been proud of the way the Milesians used his system in the construction of their city during the Roman Period.

The architect of St. Sophia in İstanbul, Isidoro , was from Miletus, too. Miletus has contributed immensely to civilization in the name of Thales, Hippodomos, Isidoro , and many others.

KUŞADASI

The Island of the Birds... If translated literally, that's what Kuşadası means in Turkish. But what Kuşadası really is, it is a heaven for the modern " nomads". The population of the town is only 13.000 in the winter and in inflates upto 300.000 in the summer. Kuşadası is a gateway to many archeological and Biblical sites. It is only few hours away from all the ancient cities of the Seven Churches of Revelation (Pergamum, Thyatira, Sardis, Smyrna, Phyledelphia, Loadicia, Ephesus). Aphrodicias, Pamukkale, Nysa, Miletus, Dydime, Prienne and many more sites can be visited on a day trip from Kuşadası. The clear blue and warm water of the Aegean sea is very inviting and very friendly on the coast of this "little" town. What people can not do when they visit Kuşadası is to resist shopping. Either a salesman at a carpet shop or a shoeshine boy will make you spend yoru money. But they would always do it in such a nice and friendly way that you would always enjoy your shopping. Once a week on Fridays, the peasents bring their most delicious fruits and vegetables and many more goodies to the 'pazar' (bazaar) and display them Like an artist would. Always enjoy your shopping. The Friday bazaars can best be described as the symphony of the colors.

There is no time to get bored in Kuşadası. If you are not siteseeing, sunbathing, swimming, or enjoying one of the Turkish baths in the town, then you would probably be either having a drink in one of the new acquired friend's shop or experiencing the rich Turkish cuisine.

The fortress on the island which welcomes the cruise boats, the Caravansarai which is still being used as a hotel as it was four hundred years ago, the picturesque city walls which now surround the narrow streets and the white washed beautiful old houses are the living monuments of the history of Kuşadası which was Ancient Neapolis, Byzantian Ania, Venetian Scala Nouva before it became Turkish under the Ottoman rule.

SELÇUK

An aquaduct which is two thousand years old and a stork which comes from two thousand miles away, the temple of a mother goddess and a house of a divine mother, the Virgin Mary, An Ottoman house built in a Roman wall, a minaret facing the Church of St. John... Selçuk is the synthesis of the cultures and the 5000 year old history.

The town is an open air museum, but when you streach out your arm you do not touch the cold marble of the statues, in this museum the people are always rice and friendly.

The tunnel of mulberry tries, the orchards of peach trees and the citrus trees, olives, figs, cotton and tabacco fields... they all paint the surrounding of this old city with a different hue of green.

Even the Byzantine fortress is very agreable with the peceful surrounding. Rather than a building built for fighting and protection, it gves am impression of a crown over the town.

Mehlika Seval,

was educated at an American girl school in İzmir, Turkey and later awarded a scholarship to study in the United States. She completed her undergraduate studies in Journalism, Public Relations, and Political Science. In 1968, she was accredited as a Guide and Lecturer by the Turkish Ministry of Culture and Tourism.

Her interest in guiding and lecturing on Anatolian Civilizations led to extensive research in History, Religion, and Traditions. Her analytical approach to cultures is the result of these studies, which she continues today as more information becomes available.

She loves her country and wants to encourage others to see, understand, and acquire a feeling for Turkey.

Guiding gives her the opportunity to share the beauty, history, and culture of her country with many people from all over the world.

CONTENTS

MİNYATÜR CATALOGUE

	1	2	3	4	5	6	7	8	9	10	11	12	13	14
Türkçe (a)					DÖNEN DERVIŞ ve Mevlana'dan öyküler									
English (b)	202 Jokes of Nasreddin HODJA	Famous TURKISH COOKERY	Principal MOSQUES of Turkey		WHIRLING DERVISHES Stories from Mevlana	Panorama of TURKEY	Turkish Flat Weaves and CARPETS	Interesting Turkish TRADES	Adıyaman Nemrut Dağı COMMAGENE	Green BURSA	MEDITERRANEAN TURKEY	ISTANBUL IN 5 DAYS	STEP BY STEP EPHESUS	Let's Visit EPHESUS
Français (c)	202 Contes de Nasreddin HODJA	CUISINE TURQUE	Principales MOSQUES de Turquie	CONVERSATION Français - Turc	DERVICHES TOURNEURS Contes de Mevlana	Panorama de TURQUIE	Tissages et TAPIS Turcs	Les mille petits METIERS de Turquie	Adıyaman Nemrut Dağı COMMAGENE	BURSA La Verte	LA TURQUIE MEDITERRANEENE		PAS A PAS EPHESE	Visitons EPHESE
Deutsch (d)	202 Witze von Nasreddin HODJA	TÜRKISCHE KÜCHE	Berühmtesten MOSCHEEN der Türkei	TÜRKISCH en GESPRAECHSBUCH für DEUTSCHSPRACHIGE	TANZENDE DERWISCHE Erzählungen von Mevlana	Panorama der TÜRKEI	Türkiche Flachwebstoffe und TEPPICHE	Interessante Türkische BERUFE	Adıyaman Nemrut Dağı KOMMAGENE		TÜRKISCHE MITTELMEER KÜSTE		Auf Schritt und Tritt EPHESOS	
Italiano (e)	202 Favole di Nasreddin HOGIA	CUCINA TURCA			DERVISCI DANZANTI Storie di Mevlana	Panorama della TURCHIA	Tessitura e TAPPETI Turchi					ISTANBUL IN 5 GIORNI		
日本語版 (f)	ナスレッディン・ホジャ 202の物語	トルコ料理				トルコ そのパノラマ						イスタンブール 5日間		
عربي (g)	نصر الدين خوجة	الطبخ التركي	المساجد التركية			تركيا								
Español (h)	Fabulas DE NASREDDIN	COCINA TURCA				Panorama de TURQUIA						ISTANBUL EN 5 DIAS		
Nederlands (k)		TURKSE KEUKEN				Panorama van TURKIJE								